the **natural** family

the natural family
bulwark of liberty

Allan C. Carlson
Paul T. Mero

Transaction Publishers
New Brunswick (U.S.A.) and London (U.K.)

Library of Congress Catalog Number: 2008020501
ISBN: 978-1-4128-0849-1
Printed in the United States of America

Library of Congress Cataloging-in-Publication Data

Carlson, Allan C.
    The natural family : bulwark of liberty / Allan C. Carlson and
  Paul T. Mero.
        p. cm.
  Originally published: Dallas : Spence Pub., 2007.
  Includes bibliographical references and index.
  ISBN 978-1-4128-0849-1 (alk. paper)
    1. Family—United States—History. I. Mero, Paul T. II. Title.

HQ535.C2816 2008
306.850973—dc22   2008020501

Contents

Introduction

I N MARCH 2005, we released "The Natural Family: A Manifesto" as a special issue of *The Family in America*. We cast the document as a cohesive statement of a pro-family worldview, with the concept of the natural family at its core. Put another way, we sought to put flesh on the skeletal concept of "the family is the natural and fundamental group unit of society," a phrase found in the Universal Declaration of Human Rights. What does this mean? What are its implications?

A manifesto is a coherent expression of a social, political, and cultural platform. A proper manifesto includes an account of history, a statement of principles, and a program of action. The classic manifesto is also universal; that is, it aspires to speak to the whole human experience, to all peoples, not just to a small community. Drawing on the *structural* examples of prior manifestos (including, yes, even the granddaddy of them all, the *Communist Manifesto*), we crafted "the story of the family," a short narrative of the life course of a natural family, and its relation to broader communities. We placed the current culture war over the family in historical context, explaining why this is "a time of crisis." In three paragraphs, we offered a clear—albeit, as it turned out, controversial—"vision" of a world restored around the "natural family" model. Among other points, it celebrates those parents who have a "full quiver" of children. We offered fifteen clear "principles" that would guide useful pro-family work in the new century and millennium, including a coherent definition of the natural family.

We then transferred these principles into four positive goals: we will build a new culture of marriage; we will welcome and celebrate more babies and larger families; we will find ways to bring mothers, fathers, and children back home; and we will create true home economies. We translated these goals into a platform of action, calling for positive new initiatives tied to the end of corrosive anti-family acts.

We explained how authentic liberty came in and through the natural family. We gave answers to charges that we expected to be leveled against us, emphasizing our optimism toward the future, our embrace of real women's rights, our celebration of science, and our quest for a sustainable human future. We explored our relationship to social and political allies, and we confessed to weaknesses that have marred past pro-family activism.

We closed by "looking forward," listing the many positive developments gathering around our vision of the hearth. We issued a special call to the younger generations, who surely hold the destiny of humankind in their hands. And we summoned all people of goodwill to join in a great campaign in favor of the natural family.

Our language and style were intentionally different. We strove to use a simple vocabulary, always choosing the one-syllable word over the multi-syllable one. We also aspired to phrasing that might—if we succeeded—be called poetic. Our focus was constantly on the ideal, rather than the mundane.

While the distribution of this thirty-five-page manifesto was limited, it stirred up strong reactions. Unmarried Americans, a nonprofit organization, called the document "un-American and abnormal."[1] Gay critic Ann Spaulding concluded that "this crowd has an unhealthy fixation on procreation."[2] The online journal *Salon.com* was somewhat more refined, calling the manifesto "a radical re-envisioning of the family unit in social and economic terms, and a sweeping prescription for the pro-family movement, one built on the 'integrity' of the home [and] autonomous family units composed exclusively of one woman, one man, and as many children as possible."[3]

A number of incidents ensued. For example, when the town council of Kanab, Utah, adopted the "vision" portion of our manifesto as a formal resolution, the wrath of the nation's liberal establishment fell on this small community of three thousand. The travel editor of the *New York Times* urged a national boycott of this tourist-dependent town, while newspapers and websites across the country condemned the "bigotry" and effrontery of this village. Hundreds of protesters descended on Kanab; many of the women wore buttons bearing the word "Quiverless."[4] Similar controversies emerged in other cities.

However, there were positive reactions as well. A columnist for the *Topeka Capital-Journal*, historian Gregory Schneider, called the manifesto "a breath of fresh air," seeking "nothing less than the restoration of the natural family, threatened as it is by [both] totalitarians and liberationists." Rabbi Daniel Lapin of Toward Tradition labelled the manifesto "nothing short of a blueprint for Western survival." Phillip Longman, with the progressive New America Foundation, warned that "secular societies that don't embrace the pro-natal, pro-family values championed by this manifesto will fade away, while societies that learn how to restore the natural fertility of the natural family will inherit the earth." Paul Russell of the Australian Family Association said that "it's rare to find a document that genuinely excites the heart and engages the mind towards a vision of the family." Clinical psychiatrist W. Glenn Jamison reported that "[t]he family is an integral human function, reflected in biological and psychological design at every level....The *Manifesto* dares to restate the obvious, in a powerful and affirmative way." And theologian R. Albert Mohler, Jr., concluded that "[t]his important document has emerged at just the right time."

From the beginning, it was our intent to turn the sparse prose of the manifesto into a book-length elaboration of the pro-family worldview. This volume is the result. The full text of the manifesto, found in the preface, is our organizing principle. Chapter one expands on the historical circumstances in which we find ourselves. In particular, it explores the sources of contemporary disorder in family systems around the globe: What went wrong—and why? Chapter two analyzes what we call the "doctrine of the natural family," examining this phrase's meaning through five qualities: as part of the created order; as imprinted on our natures; as the source of bountiful joy; as the fountain of new life; and as the bulwark of ordered liberty. The third chapter considers possible organizing principles for society other than the natural family—the individual, the church, the state, the business corporation—and explains why they do not work. Chapters four through six summon the medical, biological, psychological, and sociological evidence that supports key phrases or sentences found within the manifesto. The seventh chapter examines reasons for the ineffectiveness of pro-family witness in recent decades. And the eighth chapter makes much more specific the action agenda that follows from the manifesto's platform.

—

WE WANT TO THANK a number of persons who provided invaluable assistance in crafting both the original manifesto and this volume. Bryce Christensen, in particular, helped us gather and organize the research evidence cited in chapters four, five, and six. Joined by Kathleen Bahr, William Mattox, Robert Patterson, Brian Robertson, and Charmaine Yoest, he also took part in two editorial review sessions held in Alexandria, Virginia. All of these good people provided valued editorial suggestions and saved us from a fair number of mistakes. For those that remain, we are of course responsible.

We also thank staff members at The Howard Center for Family, Religion & Society and the Sutherland Institute for their support. Special assistance at the Howard Center came from Heidi Gee, John Howard, and Larry Jacobs. As would be particularly true for a book of this sort, we must acknowledge the faith, encouragement, and patience given by our wives, Betsy and Sally, and by our combined ten children. Finally, we gratefully acknowledge the abiding influence and legacy of the Dudley and Katherine Swim family—especially Roger Swim and Gaylord and Laurie Swim—without whom this project would never have happened. Indeed, we dedicate this book to the memory of our dear friend Gaylord, whose life exemplifies the concrete realization of the ideals advanced in this book.

ALLAN C. CARLSON & PAUL T. MERO

THE NATURAL FAMILY

The Natural Family:
A Manifesto

WHAT IS THE NATURAL FAMILY? The answer comes to the woman and the man who take the risk of turning their love into promises of lifelong devotion.

In doing so, they will discover the story of the family, at once an ideal vision and a universal reality. In our time, they will also sense crisis, for malignant forces tear at the common source of freedom, order, virtue, and children. To set things right, they need look for clear principles, open goals, and a firm course of action. They also will need to reject false charges and weak compromise. Still, through these acts they shall come to know true liberty, a rekindled hearth, and a real homecoming, for themselves and for all humankind.

THE STORY OF THE FAMILY

A young man and a young woman draw toward each other. They yearn to be as one. When they see each other, broad smiles ap-

3

pear. They sense the possibility of joy. Alone, they feel partial, incomplete. When together, they feel whole. The people among whom they live bless this bond in the celebration of marriage. The man and the woman exchange public vows with each other, and also with their kindred and neighbors, and the two become one flesh.

Over time, their joy and passion will be tested by the twists and surprises of life. They will cry together, sometimes in happiness, sometimes in sorrow. They will face sickness; they may know poverty; they could face dislocation or natural disaster; they might be torn apart by war. In times of despair or loss, they will find strength in each other. Facing death, they will feel the warm spiritual balm that heals the pain of physical separation. The conjugal bond built on fidelity, mutual duty, and respect allows both of them to achieve their full potential; they become as their Creator intended, a being complete.

This marriage creates a new family, a home, the first and fundamental unit of human society. Here, husband and wife build a small economy. They share the work of provisioning, drawing on each one's interests, strengths, and skills. They craft a home which becomes a special place on earth. In centuries past, the small farm or the artisan's shop was the usual expression of this union between the sexual and the economic. Today, the urban townhouse, apartment, or suburban home are more common. Still, the small home economy remains the vital center of daily existence.

The wife and husband also build their home as a spiritual place. They learn that family and faith are, in fact, two sides of the same coin. The vital home rests on reverence, worship, and prayer.

From this same natural union flows new human life. Children are the first end, or purpose, of marriage. The couple watches with wonder as their first baby grows within the mother. Joy and awe drive away doubt and fear as they find their love transformed into a living child. Parts of their own beings have gone into the child's making, forming a new and unique person. The new father takes on the protection of the new mother in her time of vulnerability and dependence. A happiness follows the trial of childbirth as the new mother nurses her baby and as the father caresses his first born. Receiving a child through adoption sparks similar feelings. From such amazing moments, these parents are the child's first teachers; their home, the child's first, most vital school. They pass to the child the skills of living and introduce the satisfactions of talking, reading, reasoning, and exploring the world.

Inspired by love, the couple opens its union to additional children, filling their home, and filling the earth. These parents will know the delight of watching brothers and sisters grow together. They will watch with a mix of pride and worry as their children take their first steps, attempt their first chores, take on their first responsibilities. Among the children, there will be bruised knees, quarrels over toys, lost sport contests, tears and laughter. As the children grow, they enter, by steps, a broader world. In all this, though, their parents stand as guides and guardians, and the home serves as a shelter and the focus of their common life.

Indeed, the natural family opens its home to other kin. The love and care which flow from parents to young children are mirrored in the love and care that adult children give to their aging parents. The truly rich family draws on the strengths of three or more generations. This family cares for its own. Each generation sees itself as a link in an unbroken chain, through which the family extends from and into the centuries.

In all this, the natural family opens the portals to the good life, to true happiness, even to bliss. Enmeshed in the lives of others, family members craft acts of altruism, where they make gifts without thought of self. Kindness begets kindness, shaping an economy of love. Kindred share all that they have, without expecting any return, only to receive more than they could ever have imagined. This is the love that brings radiant smiles to new mothers and gratifies fathers as they watch their children grow into young men and women of character. This is the affection that fosters charity, good works, and true community. This is the grace whereby the bereaved say farewell to those whose years on earth have been fulfilled, who have been called to another state.

A just political life also flows out of natural family homes. True sovereignty originates here. These homes are the source of ordered liberty, the fountain of real democracy, the seedbed of virtue. Neighborhoods and villages initially express this broader political life, through which families police themselves without violating the autonomy of homes. The ideal government, in this sense, is local. Even a nation "is nothing but the aggregate of the families within its borders."[1] States exist to protect families and to encourage family growth and integrity.

A TIME OF CRISIS

And yet, the natural family—*part of the created order, imprinted on our natures, the source of bountiful joy, the fountain of new life, the bulwark of ordered liberty*—stands reviled and threatened in the early twenty-first century. Foes have mounted attacks on all aspects of the natural family, from the bond of marriage to the birth of children to the true democracy of free homes. Ever more families show weaknesses and disorders. We see growing numbers of young adults rejecting the fullness and joy of marriage, choosing instead cheap substitutes or perhaps standing alone, where they are easy prey for the total state. Too many children are born outside of wedlock, ending as wards of that same state. Too few children are born inside married-couple homes, portending depopulation.

What has caused this alienation of humankind from its true nature and real home? Two basic assaults on the natural family occurred, with their roots reaching back several hundred years: in brief, the challenge of industrialism and the assault of new, family-denying ideas.

On the one hand, the triumph of industrialism brought a "great disruption"[2] or a "great transformation"[3] in human affairs. The creation of wealth accelerated under the regime of industry. Yet this real gain rested on tearing productivity away from the hearth, on a disruption of the natural ecology of family life. The primal bond of home and work appeared to dissolve into air. Family-made goods and tasks became commodities, things to be bought and sold. Centralized factories, offices, and warehouses took over the tasks of the family workshop, garden, kitchen, and storeroom. Husbands, wives, and even children were enticed out of homes and organized in factories according to the principle of efficiency. Impersonal machines undermined the natural complementarity of the sexes in productive tasks. Children were left to fend for themselves, with the perception that their families no longer guided their futures; rather, the children now looked to faceless employers.

Politicians also embraced the industrial ideal and its claims to efficiency. New laws denied children a family-centered education and put them in mass-state schools. Fertility tumbled, for "it . . . has yet to be [shown] . . . that any society can sustain stable high fertility beyond two generations of mass schooling."[4] The state also invaded the home, seizing the protection of childhood from parents through the reform school movement and later schemes to "prevent child abuse." Family households, formerly function-rich beehives of useful, productive work and mutual support, tended to become merely functionless, overnight places of rest for persons whose active lives and loyalties lay elsewhere.

More critically, new ideas emerged over the same years that rejected the natural family. Some political thinkers held that the individual standing alone was the true cell of society; that family bonds—including those between husband and wife and between mother and child—were merely the power of one selfish person over another.[5] Other theorists argued that the isolated self, the lone actor in "the state of nature," was actually oppressed by institutions such as the family and the church. In this view, the central state was made into an agent of liberation. It alone could free the enslaved individual from "the chains of tradition."[6] From these premises emerged a terrible cloud of ideologies that shared a common target: the natural family. These idea systems included socialism, feminism, communism, sexual hedonism, racial nationalism, and secular liberalism.

They coalesced, as never before, around the French Revolution. Its partisans spread these ideas—or their seeds—throughout Europe. A great war, a war over the nature of the social order, consumed the years 1789-1815. The terrible disruption of families and the deaths of millions followed.

Advocates for the natural family—figures such as Bonald[7] and Burke[8]—fought back. They defended the "little platoons" of social life, most of all the home. They rallied the ideas that would show again the necessity of the natural family. They revealed the nature of organic society to be a true democracy of free homes.

Meanwhile, a great alliance finally crushed the revolutionary force of France. In the restoration, easy divorce—introduced by the Revolution—was again banned. Families reclaimed authority. The new, growing middle class soon crafted a moral order centered around the hearth and the mother in the home. More broadly, religious leaders and social reformers worked successfully to tame the industrial impulse. The productive wonders of the factory system should be welcomed, they reasoned, but the working family could still be sheltered. They praised family-held corporations, where social and religious sentiment might soften the imperative of efficiency. And they embraced the ideal of the "family wage," through which the industrial sector could claim only one adult per family, the father, who in turn had the natural right to a living wage that would also sustain a mother and children at home in decency. Family wage regimes blossomed in Western Europe, the Americas, and Australia-New Zealand.

A century later, though, this new balance unraveled again. The horrific conflict of World War 1 began over political rivalries and fears, but its carnage yielded the unintended effects of multiplying the power of industrial managers and once more releasing those ideologies sharing a fierce hostility to the natural family. Factory production for war swept aside the claims of small property and local community. The new feminists turned away from motherhood and children and refocused on a legalistic and sterile equality. The secular liberals swept through a disheartened Europe with their post-Christian message of self-absorption. The new Malthusians pressed their grim argument that children were the cause of misery and war. And the sexual hedonists laid claim to the morals of the disenchanted young. Most terribly, communists won control of Russia in 1917 and quickly moved to eliminate the family. Five years later, the fascists triumphed in Italy, along with their elevation of state and war over home and family. In 1933, national socialism came to power in Germany and tore families apart in its quest for racial empire.

For seventy-four years (1917-91), another great conflict over the nature of the social order occurred. Those nations holding (sometimes tenuously) to a democracy built on the natural family ideal—consistently Australia, France, Great Britain, New Zealand, and the United States—engaged the totalitarians. Open conflict (sometimes involving awkward alliances) could be found during the Russian Civil War, the Second World War, and, later, in places such as Korea and Vietnam. "Cold" wars filled the years in between. Over 140 million persons perished at the hands of anti-family totalitarians.

By 1991 and the collapse of the Soviet Union, Nazism, fascism, and communism in Europe lay vanquished. The democratic, family-centered nations had won. Yet they did so only to find that the other ideas unleashed by the disaster of World War I—a leveling feminism, sexual hedonism, new Malthusianism, and militant secularism—had won control of their own homelands. They also found science careening, without moral control, into the most intimate sexual acts. Even the making of new life, the unique and vital marital task, had fallen into the "brave new world" of the lab and factory.

The temporal "hinge," it turns out, had been the mid-1960s. Among all Western nations, we find in these few years common events: new legal challenges to successful family wage systems; conscious efforts to drive the Creator out of civic life; the rapid spread of pornography; new demands for easy divorce; attacks on the meaning of "wife" and "husband"; a swelling rhetoric of "gender" and "sexual" rights; conscious state campaigns aimed at population control; steps toward easy abortion; claims of sexual revolution; rejection of the concepts of duty and long term commitment; and startling advances in the manipulation of human life. Americans call this time of moral shock and awe "the Sixties," but the campaign carried through the next decade as well.

Indeed, by 1980, the forces arrayed against the natural family could claim many victories in the Western world. Almost everywhere, abortion on demand reinforced state campaigns to discourage marriage and reduce family size. "No-fault" divorce and "marriage penalties" in tax and welfare laws weakened the very foundation of social order. The number of divorces soared. An imposition of full "gender equality" destroyed family-wage systems; the real wages of fathers fell sharply; and young mothers returned to the factories and offices with their diminishing number of children turned over to state-funded day care. "Sex education" in the schools mocked chastity and fidelity and encouraged experimentation. Homosexuality gained status as a legitimate "sexual preference." Social Security systems came to favor childlessness and to penalize larger families. Tax systems now punished childbearing within marriage while welfare states rewarded unwed motherhood. Marital fertility plummeted; illegitimate births soared. And these same forces purged the Creator from most public squares.

By the 1990s, this campaign was global. Cynically, these same forces used The International Year of the Family in 1994 to launch a series of United Nations conferences designed to tear down the natural family in developing nations as well. Cairo, Beijing, Istanbul, and Copenhagen were the arenas where they tried to impose this "post-family" order.

But those who stood against the family forgot one truth: "The institution of the home is the one anarchist institution. . . . It is the only check on the state that is bound to renew itself as eternally as the state, and more naturally than the state."[9] As the culture turned hostile, natural families jolted back to awareness. Signs of renewal came from new leaders and the growth of movements, popularly called "pro-life" and "pro-family," which arose to defend the natural family. By the early twenty-first century, these—our—movements could claim some modest gains. Yet both pro-life and pro-family movements were hampered by their reactive or defensive posture and by a reliance on political action in great central capitals.

In our time, the partisans of a "post-family" world are still on the offensive. For example, our pro-family movement has failed to restore any legal protection to marriage by some rolling-back of the "no-fault" divorce revolution. Instead, in 2007, we are in a desperate fight simply to keep the vital institution of marriage from being fitted to homosexuals. And our two movements have failed to slow the war of governments on human fertility, despite the new likelihood of a catastrophic depopulation of the developed *and* developing nations through the global "empty cradle."[10]

A VISION

And so, we advance here a new vision and a fresh statement of principles and goals appropriate for the twenty-first entury and the third millennium.

We see a world restored in line with the intent of its Creator. We envision a culture—found both locally and universally—that upholds the marriage of a woman to a man, and a man to a woman, as the central aspiration for the young. This culture affirms marriage as the best path to health, security, and fulfillment. It casts the home built on marriage as the source of true political sovereignty, the fountain of democracy. It also holds the household framed by marriage to be the primal economic unit, a place marked by rich activity, material abundance, and broad self-reliance. This culture treasures private property in family hands as the rampart of independence and liberty. It celebrates the marital sexual union as the unique source of new human life. We see these homes as open to a full quiver of children, the source of family continuity and social growth. We envision young women growing into wives, homemakers, and mothers; and we see young men growing into husbands, homebuilders, and fathers.

We see true happiness as the product of persons enmeshed in vital bonds with spouses, children, parents, and kin. We look to a landscape of family homes, lawns, and gardens busy with useful tasks and ringing with the laughter of many children. We envision parents as the first educators of their children. We see homes that also embrace extended family members who need special care due to age or infirmity. We view neighborhoods, villages, and townships as the second locus of political sovereignty. We envision a freedom of commerce that respects and serves family integrity. And we look to nation-states that hold the protection of the natural family to be their first responsibility.

OUR PRINCIPLES

To advance this vision, we advocates for the natural family assert clear principles to guide our work in the new century and millennium.

We affirm that the natural family, not the individual, is the fundamental unit of society.

We affirm the natural family to be the union of a man and a woman through marriage for the purposes of sharing love and joy, propagating children, providing their moral education, building a vital home economy, offering security in times of trouble, and binding the generations.

We affirm that the natural family is a fixed aspect of the created order, one ingrained in human nature. Distinct family systems may grow weaker or stronger, but the natural family cannot change into some new shape; nor can it be re-defined by eager social engineers.

We affirm that the natural family is the ideal, optimal, true family system. While we acknowledge varied living situations caused by circumstance or dysfunction, all other "family forms" are incomplete or are fabrications of the state.

We affirm the marital union to be the authentic sexual bond, the only one open to the natural and responsible creation of new life.

We affirm the sanctity of human life from conception to natural death; each newly conceived person holds rights to live, to grow, to be born, and to share a home with its natural parents bound by marriage.

We affirm that the natural family is prior to the state and that legitimate governments exist to shelter and encourage the natural family.

We affirm that the world is abundant in resources. The breakdown of the natural family and moral and political failure, not human "overpopulation," account for poverty, starvation, and environmental decay.

We affirm that human depopulation is the true demographic danger facing the earth in this new century. Our societies need more people, not fewer.

We affirm that women and men are equal in dignity and innate human rights, but different in function. Even if sometimes thwarted by events beyond the individual's control (or sometimes given up for a religious vocation), the calling of each boy is to become husband and father; the calling of each girl is to become wife and mother. Everything that a man does is mediated by his aptness for fatherhood. Everything that a woman does is mediated by her aptness for motherhood.[11] Culture, law, and policy should take these differences into account.

We affirm that the complementarity of the sexes is a source of strength. Men and women exhibit profound biological and psychological differences. When united in marriage, though, the whole becomes greater than the sum of the parts.

We affirm that economic determinism is false. Ideas and religious faith can prevail over material forces. Even one as powerful as industrialization can be tamed by the exercise of human will.

We affirm the "family wage" ideal of "equal pay for equal family responsibility." Compensation for work and taxation should reinforce natural family bonds.

We affirm the necessary role of private property in land, dwelling, and productive capital as the foundation of familial independence and the guarantor of democracy. In a just and good society, all families will hold real property.

And we affirm that lasting solutions to human problems rise out of families and small communities. They cannot be imposed by bureaucratic and judicial fiat. Nor can they be coerced.

OUR PLATFORM

From these principles, we draw out a simple, concrete platform for the new century and millennium. To the world, we say:

We will build a new culture of marriage, where others would define marriage out of existence.

We will welcome and celebrate more babies and larger families, where others would continue a war on human fertility.

We will find ways to bring mothers, fathers, and children back home, where others would further divide parents from their children.

And we will create true home economies, where others would subject families to the full control of big government and vast corporations.

To do these things, we must offer positive encouragements, and we must also correct the policy errors of the past. Specifically:

To build a new culture of marriage—

We will craft schooling that gives positive images of chastity, marriage, fidelity, motherhood, fatherhood, husbandry, and house-wifery. *We will end* the corruption of children through state "sex education" programs.

We will build legal and constitutional protections around marriage as the union of a man and a woman. *We will end* the war of the sexual hedonists on marriage.

We will transform social insurance, welfare, and housing programs to reinforce marriage, especially the marriage of young adults. *We will end* state incentives to live outside of marriage.

We will place the weight of the law on the side of spouses seeking to defend their marriages. *We will end* state preferences for easy divorce by repealing "no-fault" statutes.

We will recognize marriage as a true and full economic partnership. *We will end* "marriage penalties" in taxation.

We will allow private insurers to recognize the health advantages of marriage and family living, according to sound business principles. *We will end* legal discrimination against the married and child-rich.

We will empower the legal and cultural guardians of marriage and public morality. *We will end* the coarsening of our culture.

To welcome more babies within marriage—

We will praise churches and other groups that provide healthy and fertile models of family life to the young. *We will end* state programs that indoctrinate children, youth, and adults into the contraceptive mentality.

We will restore respect for life and democratic controls over abortion. *We will end* the mass slaughter of the innocents.

We will create private and public campaigns to reduce maternal and infant mortality and to improve family health. *We will end* government campaigns of population control.

We will build special protections for families, motherhood, and childhood. *We will end* the assault on these basic human rights.

We will celebrate husbands and wives who hold open their sexual lives to new children. *We will end* the manipulation and abuse of new human life in the laboratories.

We will craft generous tax deductions, exemptions, and credits that are tied to marriage and the number of children. *We will end* the oppressive taxation of family income, labor, property, and wealth.

We will create credits against payroll taxes that reward the birth of children and that build true family patrimonies. *We will end* existing social insurance incentives toward childlessness.

We will offer tax benefits to businesses that provide "natal gifts" and "child allowances" to their employees. *We will end* legal incentives that encourage business corporations to ignore families.

To bring mothers, and fathers, home—

We will ensure that stay-at-home parents enjoy at least the same state benefits offered to day care users. *We will end* all discriminations against stay-at-home parents.

We will encourage new strategies and technologies that would allow home-based employment to blossom and prosper. *We will end* policies that unfairly favor large, centralized businesses and institutions.

We will favor small property that reintegrates home and work. *We will end* taxes, financial incentives, subsidies, and zoning laws that discourage small farms and family-held businesses.

To create a true home economy—

We will allow men and women to live in harmony with their true natures. *We will end* the aggressive state promotion of androgyny.

We will encourage employers to pay a "family wage" to heads-of-households. *We will end* laws that prohibit employers from recognizing and rewarding family responsibility.

We will craft laws that protect home schools and other family-centered schools from state interference. *We will give* real control of state schools to small communities so that their focus might turn toward home and family. And *we will create* measures (such as educational tax credits) that recognize the exercise of parental responsibility. *We will end* discriminatory taxes and policies that favor mass state education of the young.

We will hold up the primacy of parental rights and hold public officials accountable for abuses of their power. *We will end* abuse of the "child-abuse" laws.

We will encourage self-sufficiency through broad property ownership, home enterprise, home gardens, and home workshops. *We will end* the culture of dependency found in the welfare state.

We will celebrate homes that are centers of useful work. *We will end* state incentives for home-building that assume, and so create, families without functions.

ON LIBERTY

Through all these tasks, we seek to advance true freedom. The partisans of a "post-family" world have taught that liberty means freedom from tradition, from religious faith, from family, from community. They also hold that freedom is a gift of the state. We deny these statements. Rather, true liberty comes from the ability of human beings, of women and men, to find their real destinies, in their ability to live in harmony with the created world. Real freedom lies in holding the power to engage in "the pursuit of happiness," which the American Founders properly understood to mean "domestic happiness," the joys of marriage and home life.[12] True liberty rests on family ownership of real, productive property. Political liberty includes freedom from the modern social engineers, who would create their own artificial orders based on social class, or racism, or the violence of androgyny (the negation of woman and man). In truth, human beings are made to be conjugal, to live in homes with vital connections to parents, spouse, and children. Authentic freedom comes in and through the natural family.

THE USUAL CHARGES

We know that certain charges will be leveled against us. Some will say that we want to turn back the clock, to restore a mythical American suburban world of the 1950s. Others will charge that we seek to subvert the rights of women or that we want to impose white, Western, Christian values on a pluralistic world. Still others will argue that we ignore science or reinforce patriarchal violence. Some will say that we block inevitable social evolution or threaten a sustainable world with too many children. So, in anticipation, let us be clear:

We do look forward with hope, while learning from the past.

It is true that we look with affection to earlier familial eras, such as "1950s America." Indeed, for the first time in one hundred years, five things happened simultaneously in America (and in Australia and parts of Western Europe, as well) during this time: the marriage rate climbed; the divorce rate fell; marital fertility soared; the equality of households increased; and measures of child well-being and adult happiness rose. These were the social achievements of "the greatest generation." We look with delight on this record, and aspire to recreate such results.

However, we also know that this specific development was a one-generation wonder. It did not last. Some children of the "baby boom" rebelled. Too often, this rebellion was foolish and destructive. Still, we find weaknesses in the family model of "1950s America." We see that it was largely confined to the white majority. Black families actually showed mounting stress in these years: a retreat from marriage; more out-of-wedlock births.[13] Also, this new suburban model—featuring long commutes for fathers and tract homes without the central places such as parks and nearby shops where mothers and youth might have found healthy community bonds—proved incomplete. Finally, we see the "companionship marriage" ideal of this time, which embraced psychological tasks to the exclusion of material and religious functions, as fragile. We can, and we will, do better.

We do believe wholeheartedly in women's rights.

Above all, we believe in rights that recognize women's unique gifts of pregnancy, birthing, and breastfeeding. The goal of androgyny, the effort to eliminate real differences between women and men, does every bit as much violence to human nature and human rights as the old efforts by the communists to create "Soviet Man" and by the Nazis to create "Aryan Man." We reject social engineering, attempts to corrupt girls and boys, to confuse women and men about their true identities. At the same time, nothing in our plat-form would prevent women from seeking and attaining as much education as they want. Nothing in our platform would prevent women from entering jobs and professions to which they aspire. We do object, however, to restrictions on the liberty of employers to recognize family relations and obligations and so reward indirectly those parents staying at home to care for their children. And we object to current attacks on the Universal Declaration of Human Rights, a document which proclaims fundamental rights to family autonomy, to a family wage for fathers, and to the special protection of mothers.[14]

We do believe that the natural family is universal, an attribute of all humankind.

We confess to holding Christian values regarding the family: the sanctity of marriage; the desire by the Creator that we be fruitful and multiply; Jesus' miracle at the wedding feast; His admonitions against adultery and divorce. And yet, we find similar views in the other great world faiths. We even find recognition of the natural family in the marriage rituals of animists.

Because it is imprinted on our natures as human beings, we know that the natural family can be grasped by all persons who open their minds to the evidence of their senses and their hearts to the promptings of their best instincts. Also, in the early twenty-first century, there is little that is "Western" about our views. The voices of the "post-family" idea are actually today's would-be "Westernizers." They are the ones who largely rule in the child-poor, aging, dying lands of "the European West." It is they who seek to poison the rest of the world with a grim, wizened culture of death. Our best friends are actually to be found in the developing world, in the Third World, in the Middle East, Africa, South Asia, South America. Our staunchest allies tend not to be white, but rather people of color. Others seek a sterile, universal darkness. We seek to liberate the whole world—including dying Europa—for light and life, for children.

We do celebrate the findings of empirical science.

Science, honestly done and honestly reported, is the friend of the natural family. The record is clear from decades of work in sociology, psychology, anthropology, sociobiology, medicine, and social history: children do best when they are born into and raised by their two natural parents. Under any other setting—including one-parent, step-parent, homosexual, cohabitating, or communal households—children predictably do worse. The married, natural-parent home brings health, wealth, and success to the offspring reared therein. It inspires the real happiness toward which we all yearn. The natural home protects children from disease, ignorance, and poverty. Science shows that these same homes give health, wealth, and joy to wives and husbands, as well. Disease, depression, and early death come to those who reject family life.[15] This result should not really cause surprise. Science, after all, is the study of the natural order. And while the Creator forgives, nature never does.

We do seek to reduce domestic violence.

All families fall short of perfection, and a few families fail. We, too, worry about domestic violence. We know that people can make bad choices, that they can fall prey to selfishness and their darker instincts. We also know that persons can live in places or times where they have few models of solid homes, few examples of good marriages. All the same, we also insist that the natural family is not the source of these human failures. The research here is clear.

Women are safest physically when married and living with their husbands. Children are best sheltered from sexual, physical and emotional abuse when they live with their married natural parents. In short, the natural family is the answer to abuse. We also know that all husbands and wives, all mothers and fathers, need to be nurtured toward and encouraged in their proper roles. These are the first tasks of all worthy social institutions.

We do believe that while distinct family systems change,
the design of the natural family never does.

Regarding the natural family, we deny any such thing as social evolution. The changes we see are either decay away from or renewal toward the one true family model. From our very origin as a unique creature on earth, we humans have been defined by the long-term bonding of a woman and a man, by their free sharing of resources, by a complementary division of labor, and by a focus on the procreation, protection, and rearing of children in stable homes.[16] History is replete with examples of distinct family systems that have grown strong and built great civilizations, only to fall to atomism, vice, and decay. Even in our Western civilization, we can identify periods of family decline and disorder, followed by successful movements of renewal.[17] It is true that the last forty years have been a time of great confusion and decay. We now sense a new summons to social rebirth.

We do seek a sustainable human future.

With sadness, we acknowledge that the neo-Malthusian impulse has succeeded in its war against children all too well. Fertility is tumbling around the globe. A majority of nations have already fallen into "the aging trap" of depopulation. As matters now stand, the predictable future is one of catastrophic population decline, economic contraction, and human tragedy. Our agenda actually represents the earth's best hope for a sustainable future.

OUR ALLIES

How do we relate to other movements or campaigns to protect the family? The conservative intellectual and political movement in America, for example, has claimed in recent decades a philosophy of "fusionism": economic conservatives holding to free market capitalism "fused" to social conservatives focused on "life" and "family" questions, or "traditional values." At times, this fusionist approach has worked well politically. And it has shown real economic results in those family businesses that successfully balance the pursuit of profit and the integrity of homes (including the homes of their employees).

Nevertheless, we also see that the interests of "big business" and families are not always compatible. Unless guided by other ideals, for example, the great corporations seek cheap labor wherever it can be found and an end to all home production, from clothing to meal preparation to child care. The whetting of appetites commonly takes precedence over family integrity in corporate advertising. As "globalization" now shows, families are not immune to capitalism's "creative destruction."

We admire and support truly free markets and equitable trade. We praise companies that grasp their long-term interest in strong homes and that craft advertising with positive family images. But we also indict legal privileges and special benefits bestowed on large corporations that buy political access and power, to the detriment of families. In addition, we point to an inherent dilemma in capitalist economics: the short-term interests of individual corporations in weak homes (places focused on consumption rather than productive tasks) and universal adult employment (mothers and fathers alike) versus the long-term interest of national economies in improved human capital. This latter term means happy, healthy, intelligent, and productive young adults, "products" that cannot be shaped by day care centers, let alone by childless homes. "Fusionist conservatism" tends to paper over such inherent tensions. We put families first. We see any economy and all of its components—from financial markets to rules of trade to the setting of wages—as servants of the natural family, not the other way around.

We also claim an alliance with the "pro-family" and "pro-life" movements of recent decades. Indeed, we might be called part of them (in modest ways). But we also see (and so confess to) weaknesses that have marred their effectiveness. Too often, individual ambitions and squabbles have prevented movement success. A narrowness of vision has led, at times, to a focus on petty questions while the truly important battles have been ignored, and so lost by default. Strategic thinking and bold moves that could transform key debates have been undone by timidity on the part of leaders and funders. Sustaining large institutions, rather than encouraging swift and effective agents, has been too common. Money, particularly "direct mail" money, has become the measure of too many things. Doctrinal and sectarian differences on important, but tangential, questions have been allowed to obscure unity on the central issues of family and life. Our foes have celebrated as old fears and suspicions between religious groups have trumped potentially powerful new alliances. The initiative on most questions has been left to the other side.

At this juncture, we do insist on "pro-family" integrity. Our true allies will accept the whole case for the natural family. One cannot affirm the natural family while also defending serial divorce or infant day care. Our real allies will be those who, as far as possible, align their own lives in accord with the created order.

We also believe that victory for the natural family will come only as we change the terms of debate and open ourselves to fresh coalitions. It is not enough to stop public recognition of "gay marriage," nor to oppose "safe-sex education" in the public schools, nor to ban partial birth abortion, nor to create optional "covenant" marriages. These gains will have no lasting effect unless the natural family is freed from the oppression of the post-family ideologues, unless we build a broad culture of marriage and life.

LOOKING FORWARD

That large task requires new ways of thinking and acting. Our vision of the hearth looks forward, not to the past, for hope and purpose. We see the vital home reborn through startling new movements such as homeschooling. We marvel at fresh inventions that portend novel bonds between home and work. We are inspired by a convergence of religious truth with the evidence of science around the vital role of the natural family. We see the prospect of a great civil alliance of religious orthodoxies, within nations and around the globe; not to compromise on doctrines held dear, but to defend our family systems from the common foe. With wonder, we find a shared happiness with people once distrusted or feared. We enjoy new friendships rooted in family ideals that cross ancient divides. We see the opportunity for an abundant world order built on the natural family.

We issue a special call to the young, those born over the last three to four decades. You are the children of a troubled age, a time of moral and social disorder. You were conceived into a culture of self-indulgence, of abortion, a culture embracing death. More than all generations before, you have known the divorce of parents. You have lived too often in places without fathers. You have been taught to deny your destinies as young women and young men. You have been forced to read books that mock marriage, motherhood, and fatherhood. Persons who should have protected you—teachers, judges, public officials—often left you as prey to moral and sexual predators. Many of you are in fact the victims of a kind of cultural rape: seduced into early sexual acts, then pushed into sterility.

And yet, you are also the ones with the power to make the world anew. Where some members of our generation helped to corrupt the world, you will be the builders. You have seen the darkness. The light now summons you. It is your time to lead, with the natural family as your standard and beacon. Banish the lies told to you. Claim your natural freedom to create true and fruitful marriages. Learn from the social renewal prompted by "the greatest generation" and call on them for special support. You have the chance to shape a world that welcomes and celebrates children. You have the ability to craft a true homecoming. Your generation holds the destiny of humankind in its hands. The hopes of all good and decent people lie with you.

THE CALL

A new spirit spreads in the world, the essence of the natural family. We call on all people of goodwill, whose hearts are open to the promptings of this spirit, to join in a great campaign. The time is close when the persecution of the natural family, when the war against children, when the assault on human nature shall end.

The enemies of the natural family grow worried. A triumph that, not so many years ago, they thought complete is no longer sure. Their fury grows. So do their attempts, ever more desperate, at coercion. Yet their mistakes also mount in number. They misread human nature. They misread the times.

We all are called to be the actors, the moral soldiers, in this drive to realize the life ordained for us by our Creator. Our foes are dying, of their own choice; we have a world to gain. Natural families of all races, nations, and creeds, let us unite.

— I —

A School of Despotism?

THE IMAGE HAS A POWER that transcends time, confession, and place. We see the young mother, face aglow from her gift of life, sure now in her purpose, a smiling, curious baby balanced on her hip, the protecting father nearby. In this simple portrait, we find essential meanings, intimations of divine intent. Through this icon, we discover beauty, order, and moral direction. This woman and man have experienced the magic moment of birth and now build a haven for their child. We grasp how this image also means renewal for extended families and communities. Here, too, we see the new dreams and possibilities of peoples and nations. Cultures that honor this picture thrive and expand; those that puzzle over or reject it wither and die.

The Natural Family: A Manifesto exists to protect and advance this image in a new century and millennium. The vital triad of mother-baby-father faces new dangers in our nation, our civilization, our world. We examine here the common crisis, drawing on both contemporary snapshots and the lessons of history. We also

29

explain how the natural family manifests itself as part of the created order, as imprinted on our natures, as the source of bountiful joy, as the fountain of new life, and as the bulwark of ordered liberty.

We begin by addressing questions: Why a manifesto? Why now?

WHY A MANIFESTO?

Communists. Humanists. Christians. All have written manifestos. This special format pushes writers toward a clarity of vision and an economy of words. It requires the expression of first principles and an honest account of historical circumstance. It demands a careful balance between the universal and the specific. It invites and engages debate.

We also offer this manifesto as a response to a true contemporary crisis in family life. As Wilfred McClay has ably summarized: "The problem is not serial divorce, nor gay marriage, nor widespread elective childlessness, nor the general disregard for the lives of the very young and very old. Those are only symptoms. The deepest problem is the loss of a generally shared vision, firmly grounded in nature, of what the family is, and why our destiny as individuals and as a society is inseparable from its proper flourishing."[1]

This document offers a distinct—and we believe true—vision of the family, one as old as time and as fresh as a wild raspberry in an Illinois June. It tells the story of the family and ties that story to a set of principles and to a cultural and political agenda for action. We appeal here in particular to the young who have faced in their early decades a steady diet of sexual titillation, rampant materialism, and narcissism. We appeal to those who grew up in a culture that denied the fundamental community of family, that twisted the state, and particularly the state's schools, into vehicles of "liberation" from the moral truths gained from centuries of human struggle, that elevated the atomistic individual to the supreme actor. We offer a different view: that in marriage men and women are made whole, and thereby gain joys beyond their understanding and duties, calling on and amplifying their gifts and dreams.

THE INDIVIDUAL AND THE STATE

The answer to "why now" carries us first into the realm of ideas, where we confront the birth of the liberal mind. This worldview took shape in Europe during the seventeenth and eighteenth centuries, with hostility toward the family evident from its inception. Rising in reaction to that century's tragic wars of Protestant against Catholic, this liberalism focused first and foremost on the individual; it looked with suspicion at the traditional, the inherited, the religious, and the natural. True liberals viewed the family as an agent of repression, fear, and adherence to a stifling past. They offered freedom to the individual. They elevated the individual to the role of supreme actor in society, the cell of the body politic, the standard by which public actions would be judged. Their world view or ideology came to dominate politics in the Western world for 250 years, and spawned reactions—socialist and fascist—which placed the liberated individual in thrall to the total state.

At its root, the liberal worldview rested on the primacy of self, the atomized individual. The English philosopher Thomas Hobbes, writing in 1642, denied the common opinion inherited from Aristotle and Thomas Aquinas that the human person was a creature born fit for society. Rather, he insisted, "all society is either for Gain, or for Glory, not so much for love of our Fellowes, as for love of our selves." Selfishness, greed, fear, and the quest for individual advantage—not mutual affection—formed the real cement of social order. Marriage had no natural basis, he argued, but was merely another contest of power, a struggle between one individual and another for advantage. Even the mother-child bond, according to Hobbes, rested on a power relationship, where women "disposed of their children at their own wills" by the right of nature and where the love of a child towards its mother is merely "an estimation by the child of the other's power."[2] Indeed, we see born here the "natural right" to abortion, over three centuries before this idea would become law in the Western world.

In the late seventeenth century, John Locke strove to put a more human face on Hobbes' natural society of individuals-in-perpetual-struggle. In his *Second Treatise on Civil Government* (1692), Locke emphasized the "equal right that every man hath to his natural freedom," a sentiment still very powerful in our time. Under this conception, though, the nature of family life was still sharply circumscribed. Regarding offspring, Locke wrote: "Children, I confess, are not born in this full state of equality, though they are born to it. Their parents *have a sort of rule and jurisdiction over them* when they come into the world . . . but it is but a temporary one." Similarly, Locke carved out only a small place for marriage as a reasonable, temporary pact for procreation and early childrearing. In his view, the marriage vow bore no intrinsic value. Indeed, as children grew able to care for themselves, "the conjugal bond dissolves of itself, and [male and female] are at liberty till Hymen, at his usual anniversary season, summons them again to choose new mates."[3] Put more directly, serial polygamy effected by casual marriage and easy divorce formed, in theory, the domestic basis of the new liberal order. Nearly three hundred years later, it also would come to dominate law and policymaking.

Writing in 1869, the influential liberal thinker John Stuart Mill reemphasized the oppressive nature of the traditional family, which he described as "a school of willfullness, overbearingness, unbounded selfish-indulgence, and a doubled-dyed and idealized selfishness." Speaking for the liberal tradition, he concluded, "The family is a school of despotism."[4]

Writing nearer to our own time, Harvard University philosopher John Rawls drove home the same point, concluding that the liberal goals of fairness and justice for individuals could never be achieved in a family-based society, where innate inequalities of gender, wealth, and parental ability were given free play. "Is the family to be abolished then?" he asked. "Taken by itself and given a certain primacy, the idea of equal opportunity inclines us in this direction."[5]

Why did these ideas have an appeal? In part, they succeeded because rigorous family life demands attention, effort, and moral alertness. Unless reinforced by a familial culture, individuals are tempted to flee the tasks and burdens of home and family.

A related, and more trenchant, stream of liberal theory has emphasized the liberating power of government relative to the family. The eighteenth century Frenchman Jean-Jacques Rousseau accepted Hobbes' contention that "children remain attached to the father only so long as they need him for their preservation." But Rousseau acknowledged the chaos that would result from a society of raw individualism. His solution was the famed "social contract," the political state, in which "each of us puts his person and all his power in common under the supreme direction of the general will." Indeed, in Rousseau's ideal society, the state would supplant even the family. As he explained, "the newly born infant, upon first opening his eyes, must gaze upon the fatherland, and until his dying day should behold nothing else."[6] These were the ideas that would animate the leaders, and the armies, of the French Revolution.

Writing in the early twentieth century, the American historian-philosopher Arthur Calhoun faithfully updated the meaning of this family-denying, state-affirming liberal vision: "The family goes back to the age of savagery, while the state belongs to the age of civilization. The modern individual is a world citizen, served by the world, and home interests can no longer be supreme."[7]

Countless twentieth century examples of the same arguments could be offered, from European sources as well as American. This view of the family as archaic, reactionary, and oppressive, and the view of the individual as the building block of society and state, has dominated the last one hundred years, transformed laws and institutions, and shaped popular culture. The triumph of this viewpoint, moreover, has both reinforced, and in turn has been reinforced by, the advance of two other powerful ideologies, or "isms," that rose in this time as well: socialism and nationalism.

Socialism, to begin with, has everything to gain from the denigration of the family. The natural family was the social unit in which the universal "dependency" problem had once been solved: Who will care for infants, the dependent young, the sick and disabled, and the elderly? How will the rewards or gains from productive labor be shared with those unable to work? For millennia, in every corner of the globe, the common, natural answer to the dependency problem has been the family, both the immediate household and extended kin. But as the liberal vision of the free-standing individual gained sway, government began taking over these functions. After a time, this transfer occurred for reasons of raw necessity, as "post-family" men and women faced crises and had nowhere to turn; the modern welfare state took form. Where primal loyalties born of the need for security had once been directed to families, those loyalties would now be to the social security state. In a "cradle-to-grave" socialist society,

Rousseau's vision would know a subtle but complete victory, and the newborn infant—from first opening her eyes until the call of death—would gaze upon and depend on the largesse of the fatherland, knowing nothing else.

Aggressive nationalism also gains as the loyalty of individuals to the family diminishes. The absolute loyalty claimed by the total state can succeed only as it destroys the reality of family autonomy. This was, for example, the inner contradiction of the supposed German National Socialist affection for families. Claiming to support motherhood and family life, the Nazis in practice destroyed the German family in their quest for empire. As historian Claudia Koonz explains in her able work *Mothers in the Fatherland*: "True, publicity exalted the family as the 'germ cell' of the nation, but social policy emptied the household of its members. Eugenic laws interfered with private choices related to marriage and children. The demand for total loyalty to the Fuhrer undercut fathers' authority. As indoctrination supplanted education, youth leaders and teachers rivaled mothers for children's devotion."[8]

The symbolic effort to drive women back to the home, so often associated with the Nazi regime, was actually abandoned in 1938 in favor of the drive for war and conquest: German women were actually forced into factories to serve the war machine. Indeed, Nazism aimed in the end at the elimination of marriage: "[World War II] accelerated Hitler's determination to establish an entirely new social order based on race and sex, with the ideal couple at its core: not a husband and wife, but a soldier and his mother, obedient to Hitler, the patriarch *über alles*."[9]

For similar reasons, Communism shared this preference for the liberation of the individual from the family. Friedrich Engels, Karl Marx's friend and collaborator, first developed this argument in his 1884 book *The Origin of the Family, Private Property and the*

State. Engels called for the family's end as an economic unit, for elimination of the concept of legitimacy, for "the reintroduction of the whole female sex into the public industries," for the collective care and rearing of children, and for "the full freedom of marriage," meaning easy and unilateral divorce.[10]

Shortly after the Bolsheviks took power in Russia in November 1917, this theoretical assault on the family became real. As the Communist leader Madame Smidovich explained, "To clear the family out of the accumulated dust of the ages we had to give it a good shakeup; this we did."[11] Some parents, "narrow and petty," failed to see the course of history and were "only interested in their own offspring." There was no room in Communist society for this "proprietary attitude." As Alexandra Kollontai wrote: "The worker-mother must learn *not* to differentiate between yours and mine; she must remember that there are only *our* children, the children of Russia's communist workers." Accordingly, children must be raised by "qualified educators" so that "the child can grow up a conscious communist who recognizes the need for solidarity, comradeship, mutual help and loyalty to the collective." And then: "In place of the individual and egoistic family, a great universal family of workers will develop, in which all the workers, men and women, will above all be comrades."[12] Indeed, by 1925, the provision of easy, unilateral divorce—"to be obtained at the [simple] request of either partner in a marriage"—had already undermined many Russian families.

In short, the secular "liberal" vision of Hobbes, Locke, Mill and Rousseau—devoted to freeing the individual from family and religious authority—led *ironically* and *inevitably* to the grander oppressions of the twentieth century, whether in the "total states" of National Socialism and Communism, or in the "welfare states" of Western Europe, North America, and Australia-New Zealand. A philosophical scheme devoted to liberty became, in the end, a blueprint for both the grand slaughters that marked the middle decades of the twentieth century and the public bankruptcies looming in the early twenty-first. Men and women have been "liberated" from meaningful ties to children, parents, and kin, in order to become servants of and dependents on the total state.

The basic liberal error lay at the beginning: the natural unit of society is not, and can never be, the individual. Rather, social order and true liberty depend on recognition of the role of *the natural family* as the fundamental unit, or cell, of society. The philosophical tradition rejected by the liberal mind in the seventeenth century—one extending from Aristotle to Thomas Aquinas—had rested on this premise. The core liberal mistake lay in separating the individual from the natural protections of the family, leaving each person easy prey for the aggrandizing nation.

THE AMERICAN EXAMPLE

The American experience offers another telling example of how this process occurred. In the beginning, the family was at the center of American political concern. It is true that the U.S. Constitution, unlike the basic laws in many other lands, makes no reference to family relations. Even its language is cast in remarkably "gender free" terms, using words such as "person" where the generic "he" might have been expected. Nevertheless, this was not due to a remarkably early outbreak of feminism among the Founders or to an assumption by them that the family is irrelevant. In fact, the family was deeply rooted in what we might call the *unwritten* Constitution of these new United States, in the cultural and social assumptions about the social order that must be present to sustain a free republic.

The Founders agreed with the ancient Roman statesman Cicero that the family household was the seedbed of virtue and of the political state. Historians underscore how the colonists had left the Old World, hoping that America would be a better setting in which to raise their true and precious "tender plants": that is, "a good place to train up children amongst sober people and to prevent the corruption of them here by the loose behavior of youths and the bad example of too many of riper years."[13] Historian James Henretta underscores how late eighteenth-century Americans raised children to "succeed them," not merely to "succeed." Rights and obligations bound together the generations: "The [family] line was more important than the individual; the patrimony was to be conserved for lineal reasons."[14]

In her investigation of the phrase "the pursuit of happiness," found in the American Declaration of Independence, the historian Jan Lewis underscores the true intent of Thomas Jefferson. Most analysts have seen this phase as a fairly insignificant substitution of "happiness" for the pursuit of "property" found in John Locke's earlier list of mankind's inalienable rights. Looking at Jefferson and his fellow Virginians, though, Lewis emphasizes that "it was within the family circle that men and women told each other to look for happiness, and there, if anywhere, that they found it." Noting the tendency of Virginians to romanticize family life, she nonetheless concludes: "Virginians who rhapsodized about the family were creating and reinforcing an article of faith for their society, a belief perhaps more central to their lives than any other. . . . Virginians often found that their ideal of the perfect family was in fact the image of their own family."[15] Along with "life" and "liberty," this pursuit of *family* happiness was at the core of American identity and purpose.[16]

In his provocative book *The Myth of American Individualism*, the political historian Barry Shain shows that "Americans in the Revolutionary era embraced a theory of the good life that is best described as reformed Protestant and communal." The American Revolution, he asserts, had more to do with the defense of "familial independence" than it did with quests for personal liberation. Americans of the founding era, Shain insists, were rooted in agrarian, religious, family-centric communities.[17] These Americans saw family households as the common source of new citizens, the places where the character traits necessary to free government would be shaped, the foundation stones of ordered liberty. Defense of *this society of households* lay with the states and the people. The U.S. Constitution assumed a nation of families. The spirit found in the Bill of Rights, especially in the Ninth and Tenth Amendments, affirmed the rights of the people and the powers of the states as bulwarks against centralized social experimentation.

Since the late nineteenth century, however, the federal government—like all modern governments—has grown massively. The doctrine of *parens patriae*, "the parenthood of the state," spawned the first examples of the American interventionist state, including an intrusive "reform school" campaign and the drive to impose "common schools" on the populace. The Fourteenth Amendment to the U.S. Constitution, initially intended to protect newly freed slaves from retribution at the state level, became instead a legal wedge for the steady expansion of federal authority at the expense of the states, and potentially of the families they had sheltered. Doing particular damage was the right of "privacy," supposedly discovered by the Supreme Court in the "emanations" and "penumbra" of the Constitution in 1965. It spawned rights to contraception, abortion, and sodomy while leveling the authentic rights of all parents, fathers in particular.

A detailed list of court cases would lead to this simple conclusion: the last 125 years might be written as the steady surrender of the Ninth and Tenth Amendments to the growing sweep of the Fourteenth and to the exercise of *parens patriae*. Today, the very size and pervasiveness of the federal government—comprising as it does over 20 percent of Gross Domestic Product and intruding into every aspect of American life—leaves the family vulnerable. The original American plan—leaving family issues to local communities and the states—no longer works in the age of a U.S. Department of Education, welfare spending, Social Security, the federal income tax, the Department of Homeland Security, and federal child care policies.

THE FAMILY IN THE INDUSTRIAL ECONOMY

That tangle of events called the "industrial revolution" also disrupted the family. Before the industrial revolution, before the rise of great cities, virtually all humankind lived in family-centered economies. The family household was the center of most productive activity. In the United States, circa 1800, about 90 percent of the free population were farmers. Most of the remaining 10 percent were family-scale artisans and shopkeepers also maintaining home gardens, family cows, and flocks of chickens. Each family raised most of its own food, made most of its own clothing, provided most of its own fuel, crafted most of its own furniture. Anthropologist Hugh Brody offers a concise summary of life on the family farm: "A family is busy in the countryside. Mother is baking bread, churning butter, attending to hens and ducks . . . preparing food for everyone. Father is in the fields, ploughing the soil, cutting wood, fixing walls, providing sustenance. Children explore and play and help and sit at the family table. Grandma or grandpa sits in a chair by the fire. Everyday is long and filled with the activities of the family. . . . There is a loyalty . . . to the tasks and expertise and duties that each member of the family undertakes . . . . The family in its farm is the family where it belongs."[18]

The industrial principles of centralization and the quest for efficiency tore through this settled way of life. The family household ceased to be the center of productive labor. Centralized factories, warehouses, and offices displaced home workshops, gardens, and storehouses. Cash exchanges pushed aside the altruistic exchanges of the family. Industrialization destroyed the ancient unity of home and work, the natural ecology of the family, which had prevailed for hundreds of generations. Mothers, fathers, and children alike were pulled into the wage-laborer ranks. Family bonds, once the source of economic strength, now stood more as obstructions to the efficient allocation of labor. The individual, unencumbered and alone, was the new ideal worker. As the English essayist G.K. Chesterton, writing in 1919, summarized: "[The family] is literally being torn in pieces, in that the husband may go to one factory, the wife to another, and the child to a third. Each will become the servant of a separate financial group, which is more and more gaining the political power of a feudal group. But whereas feudalism received the loyalty of families, the lords of the new servile state will receive only the loyalty of individuals: that is, of lonely men and even of lost children."[19]

Advertising became another vehicle for implementing this economic revolution. In whetting appetites for more industrially produced goods, it implied that residual forms of family production were inferior, and it drew family members deeper into the brave new world of consumerism. The home economics movement as crafted by Ellen Richards turned science and efficiency into the new household gods, reinforcing the turn to consumerism.

This radical change, too, might be seen as the consequence of ideas and political coercion. As Karl Polanyi argues in *The Great Transformation*, laissez-faire capitalism actually relied on state coercion designed to make human society subservient to the economic mechanism: "*Laissez faire* was not a method to achieve a thing," he wrote. "[I]t was the thing to be achieved."[20] As a later analyst influenced by Polanyi, Robert Nisbet, would explain: "*Laissez faire* . . . was brought into existence. It was brought into existence by the planned destruction of old customs, associations, villages, and other securities, by the force of the State throwing the weight of its fast-developing administrative system in favor of the new economic elements of the population. . . . There is indeed much to be said for regarding capitalism as simply the forced adjustment of economic life to the needs of the sovereign state."[21]

In the new order, the status of marriage altered. In the preindustrial order, husbands and wives had specialized in their labor according to their respective strengths and skills so that their small family enterprises might succeed. This natural complementarity reinforced their need for each other, uniting the sexual and the economic functions and giving real strength to marriage. Industrial managers, in contrast, preferred the androgynous individual, sexless, interchangeable. In this new order, men and women needed each other less than before. As an institution, marriage weakened.

The status of children also changed. In an agrarian and artisan economy, children—even small ones—were economic assets, parts of small family enterprises. Accordingly, fertility on the family farm and in the artisan's shop tended to be high. In the new order, children were either pulled away into an early—and often dangerous—economic independence (such as little girls tending the spindles in the early textile plants) or became liabilities, left at home by working parents to fend for themselves. Fertility plummeted, as actual or potential parents avoided taking on these new little burdens. Two leading analysts of modern fertility decline, Kingsley Davis writing in 1937 and John C. Caldwell writing in 2003, have both concluded that "the family is *not* indefinitely adaptable to modern society, and this explains the declining birth rate."[22]

REACTIONS: EUROPEAN AND AMERICAN

Indeed, these common products of urban-industrial "modernity"—weakened marriages and low fertility—are another reason for contemporary attention to the family. As Davis and Caldwell imply, the natural family is not an institution capable of drastic change. Rather, it is a set of relationships rooted in human nature: natural (biologically grounded) and universal (found in every healthy human society). In modernity's wake, the critical tasks became—and remain—the defense of this natural family from the negative pressures of "modernity." Specifically, family policy has meant constructing barriers around the home to limit the spread of the industrial principle and its twin, the autonomous individual, to preserve some domain of family autonomy within the coercive modern industrial order.

Early on, somewhat different approaches were tried in Europe and America, although *both* were tied to a common family ideal that would bring at least the mother and children back home. Starting around 1900, Europeans consciously set out to build family policies that would protect marriage and restore fertility to a more natural level. The first intellectually consistent efforts to lay out a family policy drew inspiration from Pope Leo XIII's 1891 encyclical *Rerum Novarum* (*The New Age*). Leo argued that "the present [industrial] age handed over the workers, each alone and defenseless, to the inhumanity of employers and the unbridled greed of competitors." Rejecting the wage theories of both laissez-faire liberalism *and* socialism, Leo called instead for an economy based on "the natural and primeval right of marriage" and "the society of the household." This family-centered economy would rest on the "most sacred law of nature that the father of a family see that his offspring are provided with all the necessities of life" and that women were "intended by nature for the work of the home . . . the education of children and the well-being of the family." This meant that any just wage must enable the father "to provide comfortably for himself, his wife, and children." Men and women stood equal in dignity and basic legal claims, but differed in social function. This goal of a "family wage" received more direct affirmation in Pope Pius XI's 1931 encyclical, *Quadragesimo Anno* (*Forty Years After*). Pius declared that "every effort must be made" to insure "that fathers of families receive a wage large enough to meet ordinary family needs adequately." He gave "merited praise to all, who with a wise and useful purpose have tried and tested various ways of adjusting the pay for work to family burdens."[23]

Inspired by Catholic social teaching, lay political leaders in France, Belgium, and other European lands proceeded to build family policy systems that would shelter families from the negative consequences of industrial organization and liberal leveling. The favored approach became "family allowances" that would recognize the disproportionate burdens carried by laborers with wives and children at home. Christian businessmen began introducing family allowances on a private basis in 1916. The French government passed laws in the early 1920s creating "equalization funds" within industries, so eliminating any incentive employers might have to avoid hiring workers with families. Corporations contributed to these funds on a per capita basis. Besides paying generous allowances for each child in a family, these funds also provided families with marriage loans, pre-natal care, midwives, visiting nurses, birth and breastfeeding bonuses, medical care for children, layettes, and fresh milk. During the late 1930s, these quasi-private funds and programs were absorbed into the French government's emerging social security program. In Belgium, a similar system provided child allowances in a manner favoring larger families: from 15 francs per month for the first child to 100 francs per month for the fifth and additional children. The government also crafted large tax deductions and credits for families with children, built a network of pre- and post-natal child health centers, and provided subsidized housing loans and rent rebates for larger families.[24]

In America, policy construction to protect families took a somewhat different course. To begin with, the label "family policy" was rarely used in a direct way; "child welfare" was the preferred moniker. Nor were there many open appeals to "pro-natalist" goals. Still, the ideal of a "family wage" also came to govern American policy formation. And the American model fostered family formation and fertility even more successfully than the French, Belgian, and other models.

Inspired by so-called "maternalist" reformers such as Julia Lathrop, Josephine Baker, and Florence Kelly, the U.S. Congress created the U.S. Children's Bureau in 1912. Lathrop, named first Chief of the Children's Bureau, laid out the guiding principles for current and future American policy: "The power to maintain a decent family living standard is the primary essential of child welfare. This means a living wage and wholesome working life for the men, a good and skillful mother at home to keep the house and comfort all within it. Society can afford no less and can afford *no exceptions*. This is a *universal* need."[25]

Pursuing the goal of "Baby Saving," the Children's Bureau also set out to reduce infant and maternal mortality and to improve early child care. The Bureau sponsored "Baby Weeks" to promote good mothering. The Smith-Lever Vocational Training Act of 1917 provided Federal funds to school districts to promote education for girls in the "household arts": This was the *first* Federal education program. The U.S. War Department introduced child allowances into military pay in 1917. The Sheppard-Towner Act of 1921, the first true federal entitlement, provided federal funds to the states for pre-natal and child health clinics and visiting nurses for pregnant and post-partum mothers.

The Great Depression of the 1930s was as much a family crisis as an economic crisis. Both American marriage and fertility rates fell sharply during the early 1930s. The New Deal, constructed in response by the Franklin D. Roosevelt administration, expanded the scope of the "family wage" ideal in federal policymaking. For example, the National Industrial Recovery Act of 1934 codified wage scales that paid men up to 30 percent more than women for the same work and that affirmed sex-defined job categories ("men's jobs" and "women's jobs") with even larger pay differentials. The Works Progress Administration, the largest government relief program, "deplored" the employment on WPA programs of women with husbands or dependent children; denounced child day care; and retrained unemployed teachers to teach homemaking and maternal skills. The Social Security Amendments of 1939 provided "homemakers' pensions" to women married to eligible men and generous "survivors" benefits to the widows and children of covered male workers. The National Housing Act created the

FHA mortgage program featuring long-term amortization, a low down-payment, and insurance protection for the lender. Joined in 1944 by the Veterans Administration (VA) mortgage program, billions of new dollars were mobilized for home construction, with over 99 percent of these government-backed mortgages targeted to young married couples. Tax reforms in 1944 and 1948 extended the marriage-friendly benefits of "income splitting" to all American homes and substantially raised the real value of the tax deduction for dependent children.[26]

Linked to these policy changes was a renewed family ethos, rooted in religious faith. Church membership and attendance rose dramatically across the country, as did the construction of new church buildings. The whole ethos of the era became marriage- and family-friendly.

The statistical results were impressive. Between 1935 and 1963, the marriage rate rose by 30 percent, the average age of first marriage fell to historic lows (age twenty-two for men; age twenty for women), the proportion of ever-married adults reached a record high (over 95 percent), and the fertility rate—after falling for 100 years—rose by 75 percent. The increase was particularly dramatic among Roman Catholics, where completed family size doubled. Following the turmoil of World War II, even the divorce rate declined between 1946 and 1960. While certainly not wholly due to public policy, it does seem clear that policy initiatives between 1912 and 1948 *did* affirm and encourage the amazing "marriage-" and "baby-booms" of mid-twentieth-century America.[27]

THE POST-FAMILY WAY

And yet, starting in the mid-1960s, these positive gains quickly disappeared. The "family model" that had undergirded policymaking in both Western Europe and the United States—the breadwinner–homemaker–child-rich family sustained by a "family wage"—entered into crisis. More specifically, a rival view of human nature focused on Rousseau's radical individual came to the fore, with a very different understanding of the human family.

One of the most systematic and influential twentieth century advocates of this new understanding was Alva Myrdal, a socialist and feminist theorist from Sweden, active from the 1930s through the mid-1970s. Her influence spread to America, then globally. A philosophical atheist, she argued that human nature was *not* biologically fixed in a created order. Rather, she believed that family structure was the product of material, environmental evolution. As economic relationships evolved, so must social relationships. A family structure inherited from agrarian times could no longer function in a modern urban environment, Myrdal said. Marriage relationships founded on the biological differences between men and women were no longer relevant to an industrial setting. The family and population crises of the early twentieth century, she insisted, were the product of a social and cultural lag behind economic change. A *new family model* was imperative. "Paid work, productive work, is now a woman's demand, and as such a social fact, which lies completely in line with general tendencies of evolution," she wrote. The so-called "traditional family" was an "abnormal situation for a child," an "almost pathological" state. Instead, "a new parenthood" was needed, one that would be part of "the evolution toward a rationalization of human life." The day care center, Myrdal wrote, not the disintegrating home, represented the new human order. In the former, small children could be rescued from the shallow views of their parents, and reprogrammed for life in an androgynous, cooperative socialist order.[28]

Alva Myrdal's arguments represent an early and relatively co-herent version of the general intellectual assault mounted against the family system in Sweden, America, and elsewhere in the developed world. Atheist, neo-Malthusian, humanist, feminist, socialist, Marxist, playboy philosopher—all could agree on a common foe: the breadwinner–homemaker–child-rich home. And starting in the mid-1960s, their assault produced policy effects. The culture of marriage—seemingly strong in the 1950s—waned. "No-fault" divorce statutes further weakened the institutional nature of marriage. Egalitarian economic policies eliminated the vitally important family wage. Population policy refocused on the so-called "population bomb," its advocates calling for dramatic reductions in family size. Day care subsidies grew; "at home" parenting drew scorn. Schools became "substitutes" for the family. Housing policies shifted to favor so-called "new family forms." Pro-family tax codes disappeared in favor of individualized taxation. And welfare systems began to penalize family inter-generational care.

THE DAMAGE

We can assess the damage that has been done. To begin with, children are vanishing. In *every* developed nation in 2005, births were insufficient to replace the existing population. In nations as diverse as Italy, Spain, Greece, Russia, and the Czech Republic, barely half the needed offspring are born. Urban economic pow-erhouses such as Hong Kong and Singapore have become virtual baby-free zones, as have American cities such as Portland and San Francisco. While babies disappear, the average age of these populations climbs. Schools are shuttered, only to reopen as elder care centers. Already, Europe resembles a vast assisted care center.

Marriage, too, is in decline. Since 1970, marriage rates have generally tumbled in every developed land. Sometimes, as in Scandinavia, cohabitation has emerged as a substitute. In other places, such as Italy and coastal China, male-female bonds of any permanence have simply disappeared. Indeed, some now claim the right to marry others of the same sex, meaning perfectly sterile unions. The image of life and hope—the triad of mother, child, and father—fades around the globe.

All the same, in crisis lies opportunity. The very phrase "natural" implies the potential for rebirth. As Chesterton suggested, the family is the one true anarchical institution, the reliable source of social renewal, the only human group that renews itself as eternally as the state, and more naturally than the state. Recent numbers suggest increases in marriage rates among the better educated and less movement toward divorce.

The Bulwark of Liberty

OUR RESPONSE TO THE SITUATION outlined in the previous chapter focuses on the natural family: its origin, its expression, and its gifts. In this manifesto, we recognize the natural family as part of the created order, imprinted on our natures, the source of bountiful joy, the fountain of new life, and the bulwark of liberty. Identifying the true character of the natural family allows us to draw out principles to guide action.

A PART OF THE CREATED ORDER

Modern debates about marriage and family frequently pit the partisans of biblical revelation against the partisans of science and evolution. We hold that the story of scripture and the evolutionary narrative actually wind up in surprising concurrence over the origin and nature of the human creature.

People of biblical faith—Jews, Christians, and Muslims alike—find the origins of the family chronicled in Genesis 1 and 2. In these chapters of scripture, God establishes marriage as an unchanging aspect of His creation, essential to the very foundation of the divine order: "So God created man in his own image, in the image of God he created him; male and female he created them. And God blessed them, and God said to them, 'Be fruitful and multiply, and fill the earth and subdue it; and have dominion over the fish of the sea and over birds of the air and over every living thing that moves upon the earth'. . . . Therefore a man leaves his father and mother and cleaves to his wife and they become one flesh."[1]

These passages affirm marriage as both sexual ("Be fruitful and multiply and fill the earth") and economic ("fill the earth and subdue it" and "have dominion over [its creatures]"). They also emphasize marriage as monogamous. As John Lierman explains, these passages underscore as well the incompleteness of the individual, as half a person, and the necessary unity of male and female: "A married couple does not fuse or transubstantiate. A married couple reconstitutes the single entity of *adam*, which subsists in male and female and is truly manifested only by male and female in concert. A married couple manifests the image of God."[2]

What does science actually teach? The founders of modern anthropology also held that marriage is an unchanging institution, universal in its basic elements and common to all humanity. As Edward Westermarck explained a century ago: "Among the lowest savages, as well as the most civilized races of men, we find the family consisting of parents and children, and the father as its protector." Marriage bound this family system together, uniting "a regulated sexual relation" with "economic obligations." According to Westermarck, special *maternal*, *paternal*, and *marital* instincts all existed, each rooted in human nature. As he explained, "the institution of marriage . . . has developed out of a primeval habit."

Certainly there were differences in the marriage systems of distinct human cultures. Nevertheless, the fundamental marriage bond did not change.[3] As a later anthropologist, George Murdock, wrote in his great 1949 survey of human cultures: "The nuclear family is a universal human social grouping." He added that "all known human societies have developed specialization and cooperation between the sexes roughly along this biologically determined line of cleavage." Murdock emphasized that "marriage exists only when the economic and the sexual are united into one relationship, and this combination only occurs in marriage. Marriage, thus defined, is found in every known human society."[4] His work pointed to marriage as natural, necessary, and unchanging.

Contemporary scientists implicitly agree. Writing in the journal *Science*, for example, paleo-anthropologist C. Owen Lovejoy argues that "the unique sexual and reproductive behavior of man"—not growth of the cortex or brain—"may be the sine qua non of human origin." The evolutionary narrative indicates that the pairing-off of male and female "hominids" into something very much like traditional marriage reaches back between three and four million years, to the time when our purported ancestors left the trees on the African savannah and started walking on two legs. As Lovejoy concludes, "both advances in material culture and the Pleistocene acceleration in brain development are sequelae to an *already established hominid character system*, which included *intensified parenting* and *social relationships, monogamous pair bonding, specialized sexual-reproductive behavior*, and *bipedality*. [This model] implies that the nuclear family and human sexual behavior may have their ultimate origin long before the dawn of the Pleistocene."[5]

Other new evidence supports this conclusion. Writing in *Evolutionary Psychology*, Ronald Immerman of Case Western Reserve

University reports that from the very beginning, our distinctly human ancestors showed a unique reproductive strategy in which a female exchanged *sexual exclusivity* for special provisioning by a male. Immerman shows that "[t]his sharing of resources from man-to-woman is a universal." Also from the dawn of the human race, it appears that *women* chose *men* because of their skills in *provisioning* and *loyalty*, rather than physical size. Women have bonded to men who reliably returned to the family circle with fresh meat or similar resources. At the same time, the ethnographic "data suggest an independent man [to]child affiliative bond which is part of *Homo* [*sapiens*] bio-cultural heritage." This trait, he notes, is not found anywhere else in the animal kingdom. Immerman again turns to evolutionary selection to explain this bond. Besides looking for reliable providers, women "were simultaneously selecting for traits which would forge a social father: a man who would form attachments—bond—with his young and who would be psychologically willing to share resources with those young."[6]

A 2003 paper featured in *The Proceedings of the National Academy of Science* examines the difference in male and female size ("sexual dimorphism") in *Australopithecus afarensis*, a human ancestor said to have lived three to four million years ago. Among mammals [including the apes], sexual dimorphism is most pronounced when sexual coupling is random or where one male accumulates numerous females. Dimorphism is least when male and female pair off in monogamous bonds. Contrary to earlier investigations, this new study finds that *Australopithecus* males and females were about the same size, no different than men and women today. This finding implies that this human ancestor was monogamous, with male and female in a permanent pair bond, "a social complex including male provisioning driven by female choice."[7]

True, it would be going too far to say that modern evolutionary theory has converged with Genesis. Important differences remain over issues such as "when" or "how" humankind arrived on earth. All the same, it would be fair to conclude that research guided by evolutionary theory does agree with the author of Genesis that from our very origin as unique creatures on earth, we humans have been defined by heterosexual monogamy involving long-term pair bonding (that is, marriage in a mother-father-child household) and the special linkage of the reproductive and the economic, a linkage in which two become one flesh. According to the scientists, the evolution of marriage occurred only once, at the beginning when "to be human" came to mean "to be marital." Other cultural variations surrounding marriage are simply details. Any "change" is the mark of cultural strengthening or weakening around a constant human model.

IMPRINTED ON OUR NATURES

While the main current of Western philosophy and social science rushed toward new forms of understanding and meaning in the late nineteenth and twentieth centuries, a dissenting school of sociology offered an alternative analysis. The first of these dissenters was the French academic, Frederic Le Play, active in the 1870s and 1880s.[8]

Le Play argued that human behavior did not follow the theoretical schemes of his liberal and socialist contempories. Rather, he identified and sought to explain the close relation between what he called *la famille soudre*—or the stem family—and historical examples of a stable, creative prosperity. This stem family, he insisted, was something more than the nuclear dyad of husband and wife, although this pair bond surely lay at its core. The stem family also embraced extended kin as meaningful, and often guiding, forces in human development. He argued that this family form "by a remarkable favor of Providence has within its very structure the beneficent qualities of the individual and those of association." It rested on ownership of the homestead and of the essential tools for economic life, solid habits of work, adherence to inherited mores, internal self-reliance in crisis, and fecundity through the welcoming of children.

Above all, Le Play insisted that the family naturally retained parental control over the basic education of children. In the stem family, children received their education at home. Even if sent to school, their most important training was moral, an education in character and judgment received by working side by side with parents. In Le Play's stem family system, father and mother also took the role of religious instructors. Properly presented, the religious principles and rules taught to children became habits, not easily broken or undermined by skepticism. Indeed, they acquired a quality of sacredness. Meanwhile, the individual would be absorbed within the family community and learn to rely, not only upon himself, but upon his family as well.

Rather than an historical curiosity, Le Play claimed to find the stem family recurring in all creative periods of human history. He found it among the Jews, the ancient Greeks, the pre-Imperial Romans, and—until recently—most of the European peoples. The stem family, he argued, combined a sense of community with opportunity for individual expression, thus avoiding the stifling oppression of the rigid patriarchal family *and* the egoistic atomism of the modern liberal system. The family is the true "cell of society" and the source of stability, progress, and authentic liberty.

Three twentieth century American sociologists based their efforts on the legacy of Le Play: Carle Zimmerman; Pitirim Sorokin; and Robert Nisbet.

Carle Zimmerman, professor of sociology at Harvard University and the founder of a distinctive American rural sociology, wrote *Family and Civilization*, which traced the course of family structures throughout the globe and across the millennia. In his classic text, *Principles of Rural-Urban Sociology*, Zimmerman followed the modern cultural crisis back to the decay of a vital rural society resting on the family.

In Zimmerman's view, the family farm—defined as "an organization of agriculture in which home, community, business, land and domestic family are institutionalized into a living unit which seeks to perpetuate itself over many generations"—constituted the critical source of social renewal, revitalizing cities that were incapable of self-renewal, either biologically or in virtue. As he put it, "these local family institutions feed the larger culture [with self-reliant and virtuous people] as the uplands feed the streams and the streams in turn the broader rivers of life."[9]

In describing the prospects for family reconstruction, Zimmerman also embraced Le Play's concept of the stem family, renaming it the domestic family. Zimmerman's other great book, *Family and Society*, analyzed in depth "a simple but relatively prosperous family" living in the American heartland. This family "has sufficient food, clothing, and shelter for all basic needs," although its members "have little money [as judged] from our commercial standards and purchase few goods." It is "strongly familistic," he continued, and "highly integrated." The family members "observe local customs rigidly. The home and the hearth are the center of their familistic enterprises." Powerful moral and religious codes govern this family form, reinforcing "regular habits of work," obedience to parents, and thrift. None of the family members are "a burden on the relief funds of the county, state, or federal agencies. On the contrary, the family stands ready to help its absent members." Above all, Zimmerman explains, the domestic-type family is an educational entity: "The family hearth is supplemented by the work of the school, so that the education of the child remains home-centered."

Zimmerman insisted that this domestic family model was not an expression of a dying or transitional past. Rather, the whole body of his work sought to show that it was a pattern of life recurring throughout time and across the globe. Indeed, he insisted that the domestic-type family was, in practice, a viable option for any age, since it provided a true harmony with the realities of human nature. A domestic-family system develops, Zimmerman said, "among all people who combine the benefits of agriculture, industry, and settled life with the commonsense idea of defending their private life from the domination of legislators, from the invasion of bureaucrats, and from the exaggerations of the manufacturing regime." Progress and harmony would only be won, he concluded, by recognizing and reinforcing the domestic-type family as the cell of society.[10]

Zimmerman's colleague in Harvard's sociology department during the 1930s and 1940s was Pitirim Sorokin, born and educated in Russia and expelled by the Bolsheviks in 1921. Like Zimmerman, Sorokin was not content with examining certain small facets of human social behavior. Rather, he sought to synthesize grand changes over time. He described the evolution of human civilizations from what he called "ideational," "idealistic," and "integral" forms to the "sensate" phase, each shift or "transmutation of values" accompanied by great and sometimes terrible crises.

Sorokin also shared with Zimmerman a debt to Frederic Le Play, accepting his concept of the stem family as the most stable, creative, and natural social form. In his best and most accessible book, *The Crisis of Our Age*, Sorokin emphasized the linkage of mounting social turmoil to the shrinkage of family size and the atrophy of family functions. Above all, he identified the family's surrender of the *educational* function as the sign of impending doom: "In the past the family was the foremost educational agency for the young. Some hundred years ago it was well-nigh the sole educator for a vast proportion of the younger generation. At the present time its educational functions have shrunk enormously . . . . In these respects the family has forfeited the greater part of its former prerogatives." To this list of abandoned functions, Sorokin added others:

[The family] is less and less a *religious* agency, where . . . its place is taken either by nothing or by Sunday schools and similar institutions. Formerly the family supplied most of the *means of subsistence* for its members. At the present time this function, too, is enormously reduced: hundreds of other agencies, including the state and philanthropic institutions, perform it. Other *economic* functions of the family have like-wise either dwindled or disappeared. . . . So it is also with *recreational* functions. Formerly the family circle took care of these. Now we go to the movies, theaters, night clubs, and the like, instead of "wasting our time at home." Formerly the family was the principal agency for mitigating one's psycho-social isolation and loneliness. Now families are small, and their members are soon scattered. . . .The result is that the family home turns into a mere 'overnight parking place.'

Sorokin was fully aware, though, that this structure could not stand. The family's loss of meaningful tasks—the move from a

"domestic family" structure toward an atomized "sensate" structure—would result in social decay, mounting crime, declining fertility, ever poorer health, and mounting state coercion merely to hold
the crumbling edifice together. He concluded in the early 1940s that
the Western world had already entered an "extraordinary" crisis, as a
corrupt late "sensate culture" gave way to disorder, immorality, and
confusion. The only feasible course was to replace "the withered
[and sterile] root of sensate culture" by a new cultural order. As
he put it: "A transformation of the forms of social relationship,
by replacing the present compulsory and contractual relationships
with purer and more godly familistic relationships, is the order of
the day. . . . Not only are they the noblest of all relationships, but
under the circumstances there is no way out of the present triumph
of barbarian force but through the realm of familistic relationships."
The remedy would be difficult, he acknowledged, but it was the
only hope for salvaging life from the darkness.[11]

The third great American sociologist in this tradition is Robert
Nisbet, best known as the author of *The Quest for Community* and
The Twilight of Authority.[12] In the latter volume, published in 1975,
Nisbet affirms Le Play's emphasis on the strength of the kinship
principle as the key determinant of "every great age, and every
great people." "We can," Nisbet says, "use the family as an almost
infallible touchstone of the material and cultural prosperity of a
people. When it is strong, closely linked with private property,
treated as the essential context of education in society, and its
sanctity recognized by law and custom, the probability is extremely
high that we shall find the rest of the social order characterized by
that subtle but puissant fusion of stability and individual mobility
which is the hallmark of great ages."[13]

According to Nisbet, the key qualities undergirding family
authority have been duty, honor, obligation, mutual aid, and protec-

tion, not the "companionship" so emphasized by liberal modernists. Nisbet joins his predecessors in stressing the overriding importance of reintegrating education into a familial framework. He notes that great peoples, resting on strong families, have existed in the past in the total absence of institutions such as the Western world's state schools and colleges. On the other hand, he continues, "we have not yet seen a great people or a great age of history resting on the school or college to the exclusion of those ties and motivations which are inseparable from kinship."

Speaking for the whole intellectual tradition founded by Le Play, Nisbet concludes with a passage of profound importance for us today. "It should be obvious," he says, "that family, not the individual, is the real molecule of society, the key link of the social chain of being. It is inconceivable to me that either intellectual growth or social order or the roots of liberty can possibly be maintained among a people unless the kinship tie is strong and has both functional significance and symbolic authority."[14]

In this summation, Nisbet is altogether correct. The family, when functioning as the *cell of society*, delivers all that is good, precious, and necessary to life as human beings. Through the appropriately labeled "conjugal act," the family is the source of new biological life—children springing up within the matrix of responsible love and care as part of a kinship community and able to grow into stable and productive participants in community life.

So understood, the family also humanizes the incentives and pressures of the modern industrial economy. The family—we must understand—is the primal economic community, where exchanges properly occur on the basis of altruism, charity, and compassion, where the pure socialist vision—"from each according to his ability; to each according to his need"—actually works. At the same time, human beings do have an instinct to innovate and to trade, barter, and specialize in tasks, which serves as a vehicle for economic growth and the creation of wealth. The family, rightly conceived, exists as the critical and only successful boundary between these two economies. It defends the small altruistic economy of the household and kin group from the misapplication of competition and individualism to familial bonds. At the same time, it defends the "market economy" by resisting the misapplication of altruistic socialism on a scale where compassion cannot work because judgments of individual need and character cannot be made. The family, when properly constructed and protected, allows us to have both economic growth and social stability, both efficiency and charity, both competition and compassion, both wealth and altruism.

At the same time, the family is the foe of *all* ideologies, those "isms" or utopian visions at war with human nature: Rousseau's liberalism; Jacobin republicanism; Marxism; fascism; feminism; Nazism; and aggressive nationalism. Claiming, through the biological roots of the order of creation, a first loyalty from individuals, the family denies the claims of every "total" ideological system. This explains, in turn, the hostility these ideologies exhibit toward the family. This small unit is the principal foe of every ideologue, every fanatic out to construct and control "a new humanity." In every case, ambitious ideologues must first destroy family sentiment and family loyalties, inspiring the innumerable political assaults the family unit has experienced since the French Revolution unleashed these evils, fully armed, on human life.

THE SOURCE OF BOUNTIFUL JOY

The most remarkable, and perhaps the most desired, human emotion is joy. While *happiness* can in certain circumstances be something of a steady state and where *ecstasy* is the nearly painful passion of a moment, joy delivers an intense and exultant experience that can last for hours, or days, before it settles into an inner peace.

The English author C.S. Lewis offers deep insight into the nature of joy. In *The Screwtape Letters*, he provides a fictional set of missives from an experienced devil to his nephew, an apprentice tempter named Wormwood. In letter 11, Screwtape divides the causes of human laughter into Joy, Fun, the Joke Proper, and Flippancy. "Fun," the senior devil notes, "is closely related to Joy—a sort of emotional froth arising from the play instinct." He acknowledges that Fun can sometimes be used to divert humans from certain tasks that "The Enemy" [God] would like them to perform. But in general, Screwtape laments, Fun is of "very little use to us. . . . in itself it has wholly undesirable tendencies; it promotes charity, courage, contentment, and many other evils."

Turning to Joy, Screwtape confesses that analysts in hell have not yet determined its nature or cause, and adds: "Something like [Joy] is expressed in much of that detestable art which the humans call Music, and something like it occurs in Heaven—a meaningless *acceleration in the rhythm of celestial experience*, quite opaque to us. Laughter of this kind does us no good and should always be discouraged. Besides, the phenomenon [of Joy] is of itself disgusting and a direct insult to the realism, dignity, and austerity of Hell."[15] Understood as an "acceleration in the rhythm of celestial experience,"Joy is indeed the way in which living humans can experience the feel, the taste, and the glow of heaven.

In this world, joy cannot be perpetual, but it is possible for joy to return, over and over again. An essential human project becomes the creation of customs and the preservation of social structures that encourage such bountiful renewal. Such customs and ways of living must give freely and generously. They must be plentiful and marked by abundance; they must be fruitful and multiply.

The natural family is the truest source of this bountiful joy, both in the marital attachment of woman and man and in the gift of marital fertility. The sixteenth century Christian reformer Martin Luther argued that procreation was the very essence of the human life in Eden before the Fall: "Truly in all nature there was no activity more excellent and more admirable than procreation. After the proclamation of the name of God it is the most important activity Adam and Eve in the state of innocence could carry on—as free from sin in doing this as they were in praising God."[16] In Luther's view, the fall of Adam and Eve into sin interrupted this potential, pure, and exuberant fertility. Even so, Luther praised each conception of a new child as an act of "wonderment . . . wholly beyond our understanding," a miracle bearing the "lovely music of nature," a faint reminder of life before the Fall: "This living together of husband and wife—that they occupy the same home, that they take care of the household, that together they produce and bring up children—is a kind of faint image and a remnant, as it were, of that blessed living together [in Eden]."[17]

While finding joy a difficult thing to quantify, social science has long affirmed that the bonds of family, the interconnectedness of marriage and children, serve as the surest predictors of life, health, and happiness. Perhaps this is the meaning of Tolstoy's famous phrase, "All happy families are like one another." In the classic 1897 study *Le Suicide*, sociologist Emile Durkheim tied the "social integration" promoted by marriage and the presence of children to low suicide rates.[18] The relationship remains strong to this day. Recent study of "the very happiest people" shows them to be "enmeshed" with others as members of strong social groups. Even among youth, "the very happy people spend the least time alone and the most time socializing." More notably, "marriage is robustly related to happiness,"[19] as is the presence of children.[20]

The possibility of happiness and joy rests, of course, within a larger matrix of sacrifices, sorrows, foregone opportunities, and trials that also mark family life. Living together in families requires that persons confront and overcome their own selfishness. All the same, it is only through this hard task that the possibility of joy opens on the far side.

THE FOUNTAIN OF NEW LIFE

Europe is dying. So are the once dynamic "Asian Tigers." America is not far behind.

In Germany and Italy, for example, more persons are buried each year than are born: populations are shrinking; and those left are—on average—getting older, much older. Even under fairly optimistic assumptions, Italy's population will fall from 57 million to 41 million by the year 2050. And most young Italians of the future will be children without brothers or sisters, aunts or uncles, or cousins: children, that is, without the bonds of kin that defined Italian social life not so long ago. Russia counts a net loss of 750,000 persons each year. By mid-century, Japan's population is expected to fall by a third.

Indeed, the United Nations itself—long a center of near-hysteria about *overpopulation*—issued a 2000 report entitled "Replacement Migration: Is It a Solution to Declining and Aging Populations?" The document warned that all of the European countries and Japan face "declining and aging populations" over the next fifty years.

Is the situation any different in the United States? Regarding overall numbers, the U.S. population continues to grow at the fairly solid rate of about one percent a year. Yet this growth occurs for two reasons: immigration remains at a high level in America, with approximately 800,000 legal entrants a year (and a net gain of another 300,000 illegals); and the out-of-wedlock birth rate has soared since 1950, to one-third of the U.S. total. If we look strictly to the marital fertility of U.S. residents, the birth rate has been cut almost in half since 1960; and the number of births within marriage has fallen by 35 percent. In short, without immigration and extra-marital births as compensations, the U.S. would be close to the same position as Europe's demographic basket cases of Italy, Spain, Germany, Russia, and Denmark.

Indeed, in all parts of the world, human fertility is declining sharply. Overall, human numbers continue to grow—the world reached six billion in 1999—but not because of high birth rates. Rather, growth comes because of better diets and longer life spans: what demographer Nicholas Eberstadt calls a "health explosion."[21] Counting our six billionth soul should have a time for celebrating a great human achievement, not for a new round of grim journalistic sermons on the tragedy of overpopulation. But such growth is a legacy from a more fertile past, and will not continue much longer. The world's total population should start shrinking by mid-century, with the Western nations far in the lead. As Phillip Longman shows, even China and India face a fertility crisis. By 2050, "China could easily be losing 20-30 percent of its population per generation. . . . Meanwhile, India's sudden drop in fertility means that its population will be aging at three times the rate of the U.S. population over the next half century."[22] Depopulation, not a mythical overpopulation, is the problem that nations face in the twenty-first century.

There appears to be six ways to understand this development. The first way is as the result of a successful conspiracy. Donald Critchlow's fine 1999 book *Intended Consequences* shows how "a small group of men and women, numbering only a few hundred," caused a revolution in American policy toward fertility, with repercussions around the globe. This group of wealthy Americans—with names including Gamble, Pillsbury, Moore, and Rockefeller—believed that war and poverty were the result of unrestrained population growth. And they looked with horror on the "baby booms" of the 1950s in the U.S., Australia, and parts of Europe, where the new suburbs filled up with three- and four-child families.

Critchlow shows how the money and influence of this group twisted popular views of population growth and large families from being "blessings" into being "dangers." They funded the research that developed the "birth control" pill. This wealthy cabal turned U.S. foreign aid into a global population control project. Their pressure and money spawned domestic U.S. birth control programs, such as Title x, and the shift in public attitudes toward abortion. Hugh Moore, Rockefeller, and Ford Foundation grants also proved instrumental in launching the feminist movement in the 1960s and the homosexual rights campaign of the 1970s; both carried out in the name of reducing fertility.[23]

Second, the commercial introduction of the birth control pill in 1965 and the legalization of abortion in most Western countries in the 1968 to 1980 period resulted in a sharp decline in the percentage of unwanted births. Among married women in the United States, the percentage of unwanted births (defined as "not wanted by mother at conception or any future time") fell from 21 percent in 1965 to 7 percent in 1982. About 40 percent of the fall in total U.S. fertility between 1963 and 1982 can be explained by this decline in unwanted children.

A third way to understand modern fertility decline is as one consequence of the ongoing retreat from marriage. Sweden and the United States offer two examples of societies that are consciously dismantling the normative institution of marriage. In the former, marriage is rapidly disappearing as an institution. In 1966, Sweden counted 61,000 marriages; by 1972, the number had fallen to 38,000; and in the 1990s, to only 25,000 a year. Back in 1960, 44 percent of Swedish women aged twenty to twenty-four were married; by 1978, the number had fallen to 19 percent; today, it is under 10 percent. Taking the place of marriage is unmarried cohabitation. As late as 1960, only one percent of Sweden couples living together were unmarried. By 1970, the figure was 7 percent. Today, the figure is over 50 percent. Some cohabiting couples do continue to produce babies. Yet their completed fertility appears to be less than half of that found among married couples.

In the United States, it is true, wedlock remains popular by comparison. Nonetheless, this country has also witnessed a significant retreat from marriage. The marriage rate for one thousand unmarried women, ages fifteen to forty-four, declined from 148 in 1960 to seventy in 2003, a fall of over 50 percent. Viewed from the other side, the number of never-married young adults has climbed dramatically. Among women in their early twenties, for example, the never-married figure climbed from 28 percent in 1960 to 75 percent in 2003. Even the "remarriage rate" for women who were previously divorced or widowed has fallen off sharply since 1965. The number of reported cohabiting couples in the United States has climbed from 523,000 in 1970 to over 5 million in 2000, a tenfold increase. And American cohabitators are even less likely to have children than their Swedish counterparts.

Fourth, contemporary fertility decline is a consequence of a new set of anti-natalist economic incentives, inherent in the transition from a one-income to a two-income family norm. In "Will U.S. Fertility Decline Toward Zero?", sociologist Joan Huber answers yes: "The most probable long-run fertility trend is continued decline, not just to ZPG but toward zero." [24] Huber argues that it was, ironically, the new demand for female labor during the baby-booming 1950s that undermined prevailing cultural assumptions about a woman's responsibility to care for children at home. During that decade, the rapid expansion of government bureaucracies increased demand for clerical workers, traditionally a female job. Similarly, the baby boom itself ironically stimulated demand for teachers and nurses, also "female" tasks.

More broadly, the very construction of the welfare state rested primarily on hiring women to do tasks (such as child care and education) that had formally been done in the home. These changes coalesced into a kind of revolution, a curious form of feminist socialism: the shriveling of the private home and a massive expansion of the state sector.

Fully politicized, this revolution soon overturned the family-friendly structures found in the economy. Title VII of the Civil Rights Act of 1964, which banned discrimination in employment on the basis of sex, undermined the American "family wage" regime. The real wages of men declined. Housing prices rose as two career families began to outbid traditional families seeking homes. Indeed, feminist ideology in collision with the facts of biological replacement "made the U.S. profoundly anti-natalist."

Huber concludes that the primary long-term effect of women's rising employment has been "to increase the perception that parenting couples are disadvantaged in comparison to non-parenting ones." The "squabble" over jobs and income is not between men and women; rather it is a zero-sum contest between parents and non-parents. Barring dramatic changes, she says, American children will disappear.

The fifth way to view depopulation is through the value-revolution which swept the Western world after 1965, marked by a retreat from religious faith. As Belgian demographer Ron Lesthaghe has

shown, recent negative changes in family formation and fertility reflect a "long-term shift in the Western ideational system"
away from the values affirmed by Christian teaching (specifically
"responsibility, sacrifice, altruism, and sanctity of long-term commitments") and toward a militant "secular individualism" focused
on the desires of the self. Put another way, secularization emerges
as a cause of contemporary fertility decline.[25]

The new "tolerance" of alternative lifestyles comes close to
excluding parenthood even as an option. Dutch Demographer Kirk
Van de Kaa notes the paradox that it was the arrival of "perfect"
contraception—the birth control pill—in 1964 which, instead of
bringing "wanted" children within marriage, produced couples who
could live outside of marriage "without fear of unwanted pregnancy
and forced marriage"[26] and perhaps subsequently make a "self-ful-
filling choice" to bear only one child. The great French historian
of childhood Philippe Aries describes "a new epoch, one in which
the child occupies a smaller place, to say the least." Between 1450
and 1900, he writes, the Europeans had expanded the place of
the child in their civilization. Levels of care improved noticeably,
and the period of childhood became something precious. But at
the twentieth century's end, Aries described the emergence of a
civilization with almost universal pre-marital sex, ubiquitous contraception, legal abortion, and record-low fertility. Aries further
concludes that the child's role is likewise "changing today, before
our very eyes. It is diminishing."[27]

Finally, demographer John Caldwell emphasizes the role of
mass state education in generating fertility decline. Based on
research in Africa and Australia, he argues that state mandated
schooling serves as the driving force behind the turn in preference
from a large to a small family and the re-engineering of the family into an entity limited in its claims. Public authorities actively

subvert parental rights and authority, substituting a state morality. Children learn that their futures lie with the modern State rather than the pre-modern family. As Caldwell summarizes, "it . . . has yet to be [shown] . . . that any society can sustain stable high fertility beyond two generations of mass [state] schooling."[28]

THE BULWARK OF LIBERTY

The terrible campaigns against marriage mounted by the Nazis and the Communists, just as the assaults on marriage launched by left liberals and socialists, reveal a common truth: the first targets of any oppressive, totalitarian regime are marriage and family. Why? G.K. Chesterton explains the reason in his powerful 1920 pamphlet *The Superstition of Divorce*: "The *ideal for which* [*marriage*] *stands in the state is liberty*. It stands for liberty for the very simple reason . . . [that] it is *the only . . . institution that is at once necessary and voluntary*. It is the only check on the state that is bound to renew itself as eternally as the state, and more naturally than the state. . . . This is the only way in which truth can ever find refuge from public persecution, and the good man survive the bad government."[29] Or, as he argued in *What's Wrong with the World*: "It may be said that this institution of the home is *the one anarchist institution*. That is to say, it is older than law, and stands outside the State. . . . The State has no tool delicate enough to deracinate the rooted habits and tangled affections of the family; the two sexes, whether happy or unhappy, are glued together too tightly for us to get the blade of a legal penknife in between them. The man and the woman are one flesh—yes, even when they are not one spirit. Man is a quadruped."[30]

Even in its most benign forms, the modern welfare state requires the full surrender of household liberty to the state. As scholars in both Sweden and America have documented, a "post-family" politics has achieved something "truly revolutionary": the near disappearance of private life and a massive expansion of the state sector. Indeed, in both Western Europe and America, the dramatic growth in female employment over the last four decades has been confined to only a few work categories: child care; health care; public education; welfare services; and other government employment. The result is that women as a group are now doing the same tasks as before, but working instead for the state rather than in their own homes. With a certain accuracy, some feminists have labelled this change as the triumph of "public patriarchy" over "private patriarchy." This new arrangement, based on massive state funding, has also allowed new household forms—which could never survive on their own—to thrive, notably the "sole-mother family" effectively married to the state.[31]

Even under the worst of governments, however, families have found ways to survive. During Nazi rule in Germany, for instance, the regime's propagandists made much of the fact that the nation's marriage rate was rising. In fact, there is good evidence suggesting that marriage had actually become an anti-Nazi act. As historian Claudia Koonz explains: "Germans who drove the marriage rates upward may well have sought an *escape* from participation in the Nazified public square."[32]

The Communist experience provides similar example. In a recent article on Uzbekistan during the period of Soviet Communist rule, the author writes: "Only traditional relationships enabled the people to survive the particularly difficult conditions which prevailed throughout the Soviet period. . . . While the sovietization of Central Asian society rocked the religious and cultural foundations of the family, its basic . . . features were preserved." The work of sheltering private society commonly fell to women. As the author notes: "I know of families where the father was a teacher of scientific atheism, while the wife said her prayers five times a day and observed 'ramadan,' so as to (as she put it) atone for her husband's sins." As the Communist regime fell and Uzbekistan regained its freedom, these traditions were still there, allowing husbands, wives, and their children to rebuild a nation.[33]

Another example of familial resistance to state coercion comes from the People's Republic of China. Compelled by Mao Tse Tung to live and work on collectivized industrial farms during the 1950s, the Chinese suffered terribly as the Communists worked to eliminate families as "fundamental habitation and production units." Thirty million died of famine between 1958 and 1961 alone. But Mao's death in 1976 brought policy changes, including introduction of the "family responsibility system." The state broke up collective farms, and families regained use of land according to their size. After meeting a quota, they could consume or sell the surplus farm produce. This system also allowed peasant families to engage in side occupations.

Results over the next fifteen years were spectacular. Farm output and rural family wealth and well-being all climbed sharply. Traditional marriage patterns reappeared after decades of suppression, as did a preference for having many children. In the more rural parts of China, three-quarters of women now wanted at least four children. Indeed, this "family responsibility system" meant rural subversion of the post-Mao leadership's other innovation: namely, the "one child per family" population policy.[34]

Moreover, Dutch scholars have documented that the imposition of Communism on Poland after 1945 did not weaken the family system there. Instead, the oppressive Communist system actually increased family solidarity: "We [found] that the importance of the family increased [under Communist rule], and that—as in

Hungary after World War II, . . . the family increased its role as the cornerstone of society. Political and social suppression can have unexpected positive effects, like the strengthening of the family."[35] As Chesterton predicted, the natural family—"the one anarchist institution"—survived, and even triumphed over totalitarian Communism, one of its great twentieth-century foes.

More broadly, persecution, disaster, even the fall of nations and civilizations cannot destroy the familial character of humankind. "In the break-up of the modern world," Chesterton observed, "the family will stand out stark and strong as it did before the beginning of history; the only thing that can really remain a loyalty, because it is also a liberty."[36]

OUR PRINCIPLES

From this perspective, we draw out principles in *The Manifesto* to serve as a guide to action. These statements also rest on other sources.

To begin with, we draw inspiration from the international movement broadly called Christian Democracy. Encouraged by writers such as Abraham Kuyper, Emmanuel Mounier, Etienne Gilson, and Etienne Borne, we focus on the concept of personalism. Each individual, this approach holds, is a unique, precious, and free moral agent. But the whole person only emerges through relationships with others, in social structures such as the family. As Gilson explained in his 1948 book *Notre Democratie*: "From his birth to his death, each man is involved in a multiplicity of *natural social structures* outside of which he could neither live nor achieve his full development. . . . Each of these groups possesses a specific organic unity; first of all, there is the family, the child's natural place of growth."[37] Such small communities are intrinsic or innate, and always reappear out of the very instincts or nature of man. They also pre-exist the state. The law does not create families; it "finds" them.

We also share this movement's understanding of the political task ahead. The great disorders of the last 150 years can be explained, in significant degree, as a consequence of the weakening of the family, as industrialism promoted by materialistic philosophers (both liberal and Marxist) has stripped away family function after family function. Policy and culture must now work to restore functions to families.[38]

In addition, we share with Christian Democracy an interest in human rights, properly understood. For example, women should enjoy basic civil legal, economic, and political rights, on par with men. Nevertheless, these rights need to be shaped around the natural differences in function that men and women exhibit in marriage and family. This can mean, for example, that motherhood should enjoy special protections and encouragements while fathers should receive a living family wage that enables mothers to remain home with their children.[39]

Finally, we share with Christian Democracy a desire for strong alliances with other faith traditions that also recognize and affirm the natural family. Following the Nazi darkness, the post World War II Christian Democratic movement worked to unite Catholic and Protestant believers and sympathetic others—including Jews and agnostics—in a defense of Christendom as a civilization with religiously infused values.[40] Without compromising our own beliefs, we too seek broad coalitions in communities, in nations, and globally, to defend and encourage the natural family.

Our principles also draw on the "family clauses" found in the Universal Declaration of Human Rights (UDHR). Most importantly, our key term, "natural family," derives from Article 16, paragraph

3, of the UDHR: "The family is the *natural* and fundamental group unit of society and is entitled to protection by society and the state." The origin of this sentence lies in the 1948 debates of the United Nations Commission on Human Rights. The arguments of the man who drafted this sentence, Charles Malik of Lebanon, are recorded in the minutes: "He [Malik] maintained that society was not composed of individuals, but of groups, of which the family was the first and most important unit; in the family circle the fundamental human freedoms and rights were originally nurtured."[41] Or as another advocate, Rene Cassin of France, argued, he "did not think it was possible to disregard human groups and to consider each person only as an individual."[42]

Alongside Article 16, paragraph 3, other clauses of the UDHR merit our support:

Regarding family autonomy, Article 12: "No one shall be subjected to arbitrary interference with his privacy, family, home or correspondence."

Regarding the right to marry, Article 16 (1): "Men and women of full age, without any limitation due to race, nationality or religion, have the right to marry and found a family. They are entitled to equal rights as to marriage, during marriage and after its dissolution." and (2): "Marriage shall be entered into only with the free and full consent of the intending spouses."

Regarding a father's right to a family wage, Article 23: "Everyone who works has the right to just and favorable remuneration ensuring for *himself* and *his* family an existence worthy of human dignity, and supplemented, if necessary, by other means of social protection."

Regarding the protection of motherhood and childhood, Article 25 (2): "Motherhood and childhood are entitled to special care and assistance."

And regarding parental rights, Article 26 (3): "Parents have a prior right to choose the kind of education that shall be given to their children."

We also draw inspiration from the documents crafted by The World Congress of Families (wcf), sponsor of fifteen regional sessions and of global assemblies in Prague (1997), Geneva (1999), and Mexico City (2004). Notably, we embrace the definition of the natural family created in May, 1998 by a wcf Working Group. Meeting in a room dating from the Second Century bc in the eternal city of Rome, the group concluded that

> the natural family is the fundamental social unit, inscribed in human nature, and centered around the voluntary union of a man and a woman in a lifelong covenant of marriage for the purposes of satisfying the longings of the human heart to give and receive love, welcoming and ensuring the full physical and emotional development of children, sharing a home that serves as the center for social, educational, economic, and spiritual life, building strong bonds among the generations to pass on a way of life that has transcendent meaning, and extending a hand of compassion to individuals and households whose circumstances fall short of these ideals.

We also have been inspired by the Declarations of the three World Congresses held to date. Representative of these Declarations, the following key statements from the Geneva Declaration (approved November 17, 1999) strongly affirm the abiding importance of the natural family:

> We assemble in this World Congress, from many national, ethnic, cultural, social and religious communities, to affirm that the natural human family is established by the Creator and essential to good society.

The natural family is the fundamental social unit, inscribed in human nature, and centered on the voluntary union of a man and a woman in the lifelong covenant of marriage.

The cornerstone of healthy family life, marriage, brings security, contentment, meaning, joy and spiritual maturity to the man and woman who enter this lifelong covenant with unselfish commitment.

The natural family provides the optimal environment for the healthy development of children.

The complementary natures of men and women are physically and psychologically self-evident.

The intrinsic worth, right to life and sanctity of life of every human person exists throughout the continuum of life, from fertilization until natural death.

Human society depends on the renewal of the human population; the true population problem is depopulation, not overpopulation.

Parents uniquely possess the authority and responsibility to direct the upbringing and education of their children.

Economic policy, both corporate and governmental, should be crafted to allow the family economy to flourish; what is good for families is good for the economy.

Government should protect and support the family, and not usurp the vital roles it plays in society.

Parents have the right to teach their religious and moral beliefs to their children and to raise them according to their religious precepts.

We include the full texts of the Geneva and Mexico City Declarations as appendices.

— 3 —

The Fundamental Unit of Society

I F YOU COULD CREATE SOCIETY the way you think it should be, what would that society be centered around? The individual? The church? The corporation? The state? Or the family?

Prior to the World Congress of Families II held in Geneva, Switzerland, November 1999, the Wirthlin Worldwide research firm surveyed people on five continents. Those in Europe, Asia, Latin America, the Middle East and Africa, and the United States, representing nineteen countries and varied cultures, religions, and socio-economic backgrounds, formed the survey group. The results cut across these cultural divisions. The Wirthlin team reported widespread support for marriage and family:

> Nearly eight in ten respondents (78%) worldwide agreed that "A family created through lawful marriage is the fundamental unit of society." Almost six in ten (57%) strongly agree with this statement. Only 15% disagree, while 7% are neutral or don't know.

79

Opinion regarding this statement is so universal that majorities in every region of the world agree. The only region where support is not over 70% is in Europe, where 54% agree and 30% disagree.

Not only do most people acknowledge that the family is central to civilization, they prefer it that way. When presented with the hypothetical possibility of creating their own society and asked to identify which institution would be central components of that society, 64% — including a majority from each region—say they would center their society around the family. Others would center their society around government (17%), the individual (17%), the church (12%), or the business community (10%).[1]

In short, the global consensus is that the natural family is the fundamental unit of society.

Of course, these alternative possibilities exist, each with its own story and claims. Appendix 1 offers an overview of their respective qualities. We consider them here as ideal types.

THE STORY OF THE INDIVIDUAL

A lone man in his own wilderness. He wakes to a morning of his own making. He surveys his environment and sees only possibilities, an extension of dreams from his sleep. The only other person in view is the man in the mirror. The day is his to capture and conquer. There is no one to get in his way. No one to interfere. No one to cast judgment, to impose a threat, to make afraid. Just a lone man with limitless imagination to claim the day.

He will ponder in the still of the morning, "Should I go fishing? Should I build a house? Should I comb my hair? Should I invent a cure for cancer?" The mattress upon which he still sits feels very comfortable. He could just lay the day away. There is no pressure to do anything. He might be tempted to act basely. There is certainly no other person for whom to do anything. There will be no one calling him, no one knocking on the door, no mail to open, no one to impress.

The world he meets he faces alone. He will cry alone and face sickness alone. Life has very little meaning because, for him, life has very little contrast. While he might smile, he will not feel joy. While he might weep, he will not feel sadness. The lone man cannot provide meaning, context, or definition to his life. His perspective is one-dimensional. His ideals, if any, are dull. The lone man might do anything, but he will rarely recognize what he has done.

But even a lone man must survive—his one true purpose in life. He must be fed. He must be sheltered. He must be safe. Furthermore, he might choose to be comfortable, as he has been in the bed of his own making. He begins the day with "must" and then moves on to "might."

Happiness? A full belly. Progress? The sure prospect of a full belly. Safety? Protection from the elements. Comfort? Protection from the elements by degree. And so he ventures out of bed. His quest is simple—what will it take to stay alive today? On a good day, if he is motivated, his quest might include a larger thought— what will it take to stay alive this week? Or, on achieving a degree of comfort, how can that level be maintained?

In an isolated world, our lone man is truly on his own. As if booted singly from a terrestrial Garden of Eden, he looks warily at the trials of a unknown world facing him and sees only a vast nothingness. Or, undaunted, he might instead see unlimited re-sources and no one preventing him from consuming them. Either way, he is both captain and king of his destiny, not to mention both slave and laborer.

There is a little of the lone man in all of us. It is what makes us selfish, narrow-minded, impatient, prideful, carnal, and otherwise self-absorbed. It also can drive us habitually to get what we need and want out of life. In consequence, any society focused chiefly upon the individual will soon confront a unique set of problems and promises.

While few people actually live isolated from other human beings, the ideology and psychology of atomistic individualism creates social frameworks of isolation. That is, amidst the masses, the atomistic individual is hard pressed to cope effectively day in and day out because at every turn his internal wiring runs contrary to social conformity and function. And even when conformity is in his best interests, he fails to recognize that beyond mere conformity lies cooperation; self-interest simply offers no perspective on such cooperation, let alone the productive values of a working community. Again, he is left to operate within a social framework without understanding its meaning, context, and definition.

Not conforming to the natural order around him nags his individualist psyche. "Why is my approach wrong? Why must I conform? Surely I am not isolated. I have friends and associates—those other individuals who help me get what I need and want out of life. Besides, I am free and they are free and together we are a free people. In fact, our society is both free and prosperous because it is interdependent, requiring all individuals to work toward their own best interests, and cooperative, for without each other we would truly be left a lone man in our own wilderness."

Within this psychological framework he is economic man, if he is anything. This is his obvious strength to a society based on the individual. His survival instinct drives him to care for himself. As an economic creature, he says that when everyone is looking out for his or her own self-interest, such selfish behavior will also serve the interests of others. A man who knows how to build homes needs to eat while another man has food but no home. Their respective self-interests allow them to trade a skill for a commodity and satisfy both needs. This "community of self-interest" seems to have all the answers. It seems to explain all sorts of behavior, social as well as economic. Individuals marry out of self-interest; they commune spiritually out of self-interest; they organize politically out of self-interest; they build societies out of self-interest. The "invisible hand" really seems to work!

So we ask, if everyone is getting what they desire out of self-interest, then why not build a society on the fundamental unit of the atomistic individual? The answer to this question might be surprising to some people; no doubt it will sound as simplistic as its counter-claim. The answer is that such a community of self-interest cannot preserve its freedom, over the long haul.

The individual is incomplete. And a society of individuals is just as incomplete. Contrary to its proponents' claims, a society based upon the individual is not like a puzzle in which all of the pieces come together neatly to complete a picture. When everyone has a different vision, there is no vision. Rather, the picture it creates is vague and chaotic. While this situation offers incentives for every person to work out the possibilities in each new reality, it fails to offer peace, stability, order, and function. It offers its participants a very fragile house of cards built to collapse in the end. All persons become laws unto themselves, self-justified, because every vision has some merit.

The key to understanding individualism's innate weakness is to grasp its innate strength: such individualism is simply a choice, as to how each of us will live in an existence that transcends our individual life. It is a choice of how to be purposeful and how to belong. And this is why we value our individualism so highly—it is the pathway to other possible lives. We value our ability to choose, but to choose something more than the self, not something less. This is especially so as we contemplate building a society.

In a world where the individual is the fundamental unit, people are socially isolated. Culturally, they are narcissistic. Their art and literature reflect their self-absorption—a world of autobiographies and self-portraits—literally reflective but not genuine. Politically, they are very utilitarian or, we might say today, libertarian. As the conservative scholar Russell Kirk once observed, "We flawed human creatures are sufficiently selfish already, without being exhorted to pursue selfishness on principle."

To conclude this brief analysis of how the story of the individual contrasts with the story of the family, let us turn to a geological metaphor. Sand is nothing more than atomized stone. Though substantial in the aggregate, it is no more than the accidental product of stones and shells as they slowly disintegrate.

Individualism as a force is no more than the atomization of the family unit. Individualism is the sand; family is the stone. A society built upon the foundation of atomized individualism will never be able to sustain the weight of human experience. Family is the fundamental unit of society for good reason; it is the stone upon which humans can rely even as waves break upon it. We might think we can build our human institutions from the sand of individualism. But no matter how high we build our sand castles, they dissolve in the first real storm.

THE STORY OF THE CHURCH

The church, meaning here an organized structure focused on the worship of God and the promotion of the faith, is another potential center for social organization. As a reflection or, perhaps, a conduit for the divine, the church can claim special authority. This might even include privileged communication with the Creator.

Relative to individuals, the church can motivate persons toward sacrifice, through the subordination of selfish interests to a common creed. With an ultimate grounding in faith rather than in reason, the church can show a special authority and mobilize its followers toward effective action.

Concerning morality, the church is ideally suited to bring out the good (or at least the better) in all people. It inspires and channels charity and good works, alleviating the needs of the poor, the sick, and the suffering. It creates educational structures that rest on solid virtues and teach wisdom and heritage. By insisting on self-discipline, the church motivates its followers to good health and social stability. As a community of saints, it inspires happiness.

Relative to the economy, the church transcends the narrow views and selfish demeanor of *homo economicus*. The divine economy has a different purpose and structure in which the marketplace is irrelevant and money holds no value. Instead, the church relies on altruism, or selfless giving based on love and duty. Rejecting raw materialism, the church focuses instead on matters of the spirit. In place of money, the church delivers compassion, charity, and personal care.

Regarding order, the church holds to an orthodoxy that changes only slowly, if at all. Adherence to core doctrines alleviates uncertainties, doubts, unhappiness. Rejecting rival truth claims actually frees individuals to live in *their* version of truth, with a certitude that brings inner peace.

All of these qualities reinforce the potential role of the church as the fundamental unit of society. On further examination, though, such a claim falters before the lessons of history, and of scripture itself.

Regarding the latter, the Book of Genesis—sacred to Jews, Christians, and Muslims alike—clearly shows the *family* as pre-existing the church. The creation of humankind in the image of God, "male and female created he them" (Genesis 1:27), the admonition that they "be fruitful, and multiply, and replenish the earth (1:28)," the charge that a man "shall leave his father and his mother and shall cleave unto his wife: and they shall be one flesh" (2:24), and the conception and bearing of children (4:1-2) all occurred well before men "began . . . to call upon the name of the Lord" (4:26).

We also have an historical record of attempts to build a City of God on earth. Many of those that worked for a time were marked by a modest size and geographic isolation: the Massachusetts Bay Colony of the early seventeenth century, and the Amana Colonies of Iowa and the United Order of the Mormons, both founded in the nineteenth century. Such experiments worked, and even thrived, for several generations. Eventually, though, they integrated back into a larger and more complicated social order. In addition, some small experiments in building a City of God ended in apparent exploitation and violence: remember Jonestown in Guyana and the Branch Davidians in Texas.

More important have been efforts to build national or imperial projects premised on a practical union between state and church. The Holy Roman Empire of Charlemagne, the Hapsburg Empire of Charles v, the Ottoman Empire of the Caliphs, and the contemporary Kingdom of Saudi Arabia—all can claim impressive achievements and world-historic influence. And yet, all have proven vulnerable to another force: dissent. The close union of church and state mandates the steady suppression of heresy. In Medieval Europe, violent campaigns targeted the Albigensians, the Hussites, and others. The Ottomans allowed Jews and Christians to exist as tribute-paying communities, stripped of political influence and unable to proselytize. The Saudis prohibit any non-Islamic activity on their soil.

Such structures cannot survive in the modern world. They are incapable of accommodating free thought, innovation, diversity, or real democracy. The Holy Roman, Hapsburg, and Ottoman Empires are gone; the Kingdom of Saudi Arabia now falls victim to its internal contradictions. Indeed, the pervasiveness of organized religion in this world actually proves the unlikelihood of a city of God—too many gods, too many prophets, too many doctrines, and too few like-minded adherents.

All the same, a city of God can and does exist in the family. The family is a perfect home for God. Organized religion then becomes a true complement to society and an effective facilitator of religious expression. Religious expression has no limits, and differences in the ways families express their religious beliefs become strengths for the community. The family provides the best opportunity for religion to flourish—it allows for diversity of belief and encourages communities of belief. It provides a proving ground of faith for children to test religious values and ideals safely.

It is true that religious expression in some families is a hard and austere experience for children. However, the alternative—the lack of any religious experience—usually sends children into an emotional and social tailspin.

The power of religious faith centered in the family comes as no surprise. The family is prior to organized religion. The latter was created, in part, to serve the former. The story of the church recognizes an ordered universe. The family is at the center of that universe. It is the nearest point to heaven in our fallen world.

THE STORY OF THE CORPORATION

Unlike other possible organizing units of society, the story of the corporation is direct, and it comes in two parts: the transaction and the money. To establish the corporation as the fundamental unit of society is to base society's entire existence on the free exchange of goods and services and the quest for wealth. We might be tempted to say at this point that neither purpose is bad in itself, but we should reserve judgment on this point because it will become crucial in discerning exactly why the corporation fails as a fundamental unit.

Like the story of the church, the story of the corporation can be framed by the walls it occupies. It too has its cathedrals and towers, its prophets and seers, its organization and policies. Even so, uniquely different within this particular story is the identity of those it serves. Almost uniformly throughout the world, the corporation is established with a governing board of directors whose sole purpose is to serve its shareholders, and to do so in only one way: to make them money.[2]

It is rather an ingenuous model. Shareholders, the investors and owners, willingly part with their capital and place it in the hands of the board of directors. They do so with confidence because the directors are capable men and women who will care for the operation and maintenance of the business. The shareholders (again, the owners of the business) are not burdened with the day to day management of their investment. They simply turn their money over to the corporation and it serves them. Moreover, the shareholders typically are not liable for anything that goes awry. They risk one thing and one thing only—their money.

But the ingenuity of the model does not stop there. The corporation is a legal person, in some respects independent of its owners. In fact, its owners, even the most important among them, will come and go, die even, and the corporation is structured to outlive them all. A corporation is an artificial person and, in the United States as in most of the Western world, it is protected by due process and equal protection. It has rights.

Its story can be summed up neatly by United States Supreme Court Chief Justice John Marshall:

> A corporation is an artificial being, invisible, and existing only in contemplation of law. Being the mere creation of law, it possesses only those properties which the charter of its creation confers upon it . . . These are such as are supposed best calculated to effect the object for which it was created. Among the most important are immortality and if the expression may be allowed, individuality; properties by which a perpetual succession of many persons are considered as the same, so that they may act as a single individual. A corporation manages its own affairs, and holds property without the hazardous and endless necessity of perpetual conveyance for the purpose of transmitting it from hand to hand. It is chiefly for the purpose of clothing bodies of men, in succession, with these qualities and capacities, that corporations were invented, and are in use. By these means, a perpetual succession of individuals are capable of acting for the promotion of the particular object, like one immortal being.[3]

Immortality: a remarkably solid basis for the future. The corporation has a charter, a purpose, and functions for its associates to fulfill; it is organized and governed strictly through its by-laws. Better yet, it is uncomplicated. All those involved know their roles, for despite a necessary division of labor within the corporation, their varied tasks collectively become one: to make money.

But there is something more to the story of the corporation than just money. This story is incomplete without an understanding of its remarkable allegiance to transactions. Advocates of the corporation often defend this allegiance as essential to the integrity of the free flow of goods and services. Even in competition among its own kind, corporations will stand unified in defense of this free flow. The freedom to transact should not be encumbered. If making money is its primary object, then the ability to transact must be held inviolate. In many respects the corporation represents liberty—the power to transact freely, to work, to make money, and to prosper. Add to this liberty its organizational prowess and a keen argument could be made that the corporation is an ideal basis for an aspiring society.

While the corporation has blessed the economies of men, it would be extremely short-sighted to assume that it has the where-withal to carry the weight of being the fundamental social unit. Indeed, its problems here are many-fold, not the least of which is the counter-social behavior for which it creates incentives.

Withhold judgment for the time about the innate goodness of the corporation's two purposes, maintaining complete freedom of transaction and making money. After all, making money through honest work or trade is a good thing and transactions facilitate it. But the innate goodness of this two-fold purpose does not exist in a vacuum. It must compete with other reasonable purposes. When Milton Friedman said "the business of business is business," he authoritatively sided with the two-fold purpose to the exclusion of others. For instance, the business of business is not promoting social welfare. The business of business is not maintaining a family. The business of business is not even primarily advancing the well-being of its employees and administrators. What the esteemed economist was saying is that the business of business is to make money for the shareholders. In a society so organized, the work of care is done by those who do it for money. Those without money receive no care.

The other half of this dual purpose appears in a similar context. The transaction facilitates the making of money and the freer our transactions, the more money that can be made. It is important to note that for the transaction to maximize its value, it must be completely unrestrained. This is important, for it reveals that the transaction alone is the value, not what is being bought and sold. It recognizes no distinction between oranges and guns, no distinctions between human flesh and poultry. The price of a good or service is a function of a corporate "bottom line," but the real value of anything is whether or not it can be part of a transaction. If distinctions are drawn between commodities, it is not the result of some kind of corporate discernment, only some external proscription. There is no incentive for a corporation to proscribe, for instance, the sale of pornography. It is a commodity like any other to be bought and sold. Such a prohibition must be handed down from elsewhere in society.

Initially we held to the proposition that to establish the corporation as the fundamental unit of society would be to base society's entire existence on the free exchange of goods and services and the quest for money. And then we were tempted to say that neither purpose was bad in and of itself, but that we should reserve judgment. This is why. Like the goodness of the individual, the goodness of the corporation depends ultimately on choice—a choice as to how we will lead and conduct our lives according to purposes much greater than simply making money and trading. However, life itself is about more than making money. Any healthy society will reflect this broader definition of life. As such, the corporation is only a part of this broader life, and certainly not its center.

Were we to place the corporation at the center of our society, we would find ourselves in a world lacking in order, beauty, and grace. We would find ourselves competing with other family members and neighbors in a setting of social Darwinism that would divide rather than unify. Our culture, too, would be fiercely competitive—creating a Marxist portrait of haves and have-nots painted not only on an economic canvas but everywhere—an environment in which money alone made something right, or its lack made something wrong. Politically, we would function in a perverse meritocracy, claiming to reward meritorious achievement but, as in *The Richest Man in Babylon*, only finding a standard in our ability to make and handle money. And imagine our spiritual lives—the profit motive as religious doctrine?

We see the great value of the corporation. It creates jobs, wealth, and many other benefits. We recognize that money is required in this life and that we must have sufficient sums for our needs. We appreciate the liberty afforded transactions within the story of the corporation. We see the value in creating incentives for industry and competition. What we do not see is why these qualities should be the center of our lives and the foundation upon which we build everything else.

The story of the corporation is much too narrow to drive a healthy society. Only the natural family can do that. As much as families can benefit from the wealth generated by corporations, the value of such surplus does not come close to the bounty required for lasting peace and happiness in a context of ordered liberty.

THE STORY OF THE STATE

Try to paint a picture of the state as the fundamental unit of society. Would it look like the *Republic*? *Leviathan*? *Animal Farm*? *1984*?

The Communist Manifesto? Mein Kampf? A Brave New World? Or would its shades and hues be more subtle? Like perfectly planned communities? Government schools? A social welfare program? Public mass transit? The New Deal? The Fair Deal? The Great Society? Or would such a portrait be a series of revolutionary representations? The French Revolution? The Russian Revolution? The Asian genocides from Mao to Pol Pot? Mass starvations in Eastern Europe? The gas and torture chambers in Nazi concentration camps?

Of course, these portraits beg a very important question. Is there one among them, or any other we can recall, that depicts a productive, healthy, peaceful, and joyous picture of community life and personal freedom? And if not, why?

The story of the state should not be confused with the need for government. Purposeful lives require governing, and when formalized, we call such a task government. There is self-government, family government, contractual government, local or neighborhood government, state or provincial government, federal or national government, and even international government. The story of the state actually separates the spiritual from the physical, essence from matter. This story is the tale of a harsh reality—unforgiving, uniform, relentless, given to extremes, and as intrusive as a small piece of stone in our shoe.

This story is not a pretty one, no matter how it is told. But it always begins in the same place—the quest for perfection. And it always ends the same way—in failure. The narrative in between goes something like this.

This abstract state lies in waiting, the would-be servant of the people. It will do no more or no less than what is requested of it. Of course, it is eager to help; it is just waiting to be asked. Not impatiently, mind you. It understands its place, role, and functions perfectly. It would never pretend to assume a responsibility not delegated to it by the people.

However, it does observe the world around it. It sees disorder and chaos. It sees need and want. It sees unhappiness and disease. It sees starvation and poverty, classes and conscience, waste and destruction, greed and envy. It sees the crushing burden of tradition. And it asks why such things must exist? Surely it could be called upon to intercede, to fix what is broken. After all, it has the power to fix anything. So there it sits perplexed, but patient—why are the people not calling on it to help?

It sees that there is and always has been a sinister force behind nearly every social problem. This conspirator against perfectibility goes by many names—agency, free will, liberty—but the state knows it by its most pejorative expression: the freedom to choose, or, simply, choice. It wonders why the people cannot see this self-evident problem. To be able to do what you want to do is to possess exactly the kind of power needed to correct so many problems. Yet, to see that power reduced to the individual whims of the people is inefficient. People could be so much better served by letting the state exercise that power by dictating all decisions. In fact, allowing this control only makes sense; it is efficient.

Alas, the state's patience pays off. Finally, a few people emerge who see the world the way it does. Better yet, they see the value of the state in finding solutions to their various problems. Slowly but steadily come the flow of requests for assistance: "People are much too different. What can the state do to help correct this inconsistency? People are not diverse enough. How can the state encourage multiculturalism? Some people have too much money while others go without the basics of life. What can the state do to correct this inequality? Surely some people are brighter and more intelligent than others. How can the state help the others understand what is good for them? Religiously-based morality is too exclusionary. How can the state rid itself of any such influences? People are not morally sensitive to the circumstances of others. How can the state shape an acceptable public morality?"

The state feels liberated to do what it was created to do. It can help. Very soon, things appear to get done. The problems seem like they are being addressed. The trains run on time. The people are grateful for answers to their problems, especially their money problems. The state is more than happy to step in to fill the inadequacies of the people.

Sooner rather than later, however, the apparent answers begin to fall short. The state struggles with more solutions. Perhaps not enough resources have been allocated to address the problem properly? Perhaps the right operatives were not in place to execute the "recovery plan"? Perhaps the people have not transferred enough authority to government?

Then the real answer emerges. People are the problem. Of course! Perfectibility is not possible so long as people are allowed to choose activities and behaviors that run counter to the quest for efficiency. The state ponders the matter. It faces the ultimate dilemma—how does it effectively deliver to the people complete safety and optimal welfare without the ability to control their lives and decisions?

It is at this point that the story of the state turns ugly. This is the point of the final option—it must save the people from themselves and it must do so with rapidity and force. A helping hand becomes a back hand. The servant becomes the master. The state becomes the fundamental unit of society. The people are now the problem; all will suffer; some must die.

Choosing this path is deceptively easy. After all, the state is only trying to help. And, by the way, the people asked for the help.

The state is only doing what the people asked it to do. The requests were reasonable enough—work for the common good, for decency, for the common man, for the provision of order, and for the unity of the people. We must all live together in peace. This can only be accomplished if the state is allowed to fulfill its purpose, and if people are not allowed to choose their own existence.

This story of the state has been lived and relived, tried over and again with the result always being failure. To place the state as the fundamental unit of society is to dehumanize people. No longer are people the reason for, or the purpose of, life. Perfection becomes the end game—a game lost even before it is played.

THE MIXED UNIT

In answering our initial question—"If you could create society the way you think it should be, what would that society be centered around?"—we might be forced to ask another obvious one. Must we choose just one axis? This is a very reasonable question, reflecting an obvious sentiment. Perhaps there is a more eclectic, menu-driven way of settling upon what combination of center-points actually work best. Why must we be forced to choose one over another? After all, we need each of these organizing principles in our lives. So, if we need the strengths of each, why not craft a blended center-point taking the best from each? What is the result?

Let us define a center-point utilizing the primary strength of each (you can craft a mixed unit however you like using the matrix in Appendix 1): the economic power of the individual (the "invisible hand"), the cultural power of the family (traditional and generational), the social power of the church (communal), the spiritual power of the corporation (yes, spiritual power—the "profit motive"), and the political power of the state (its coercive power).

Immediately, we run into a dilemma. The invisible hand runs head long into the coercive power of the state. And then the communal, or cooperative, sociality of religion, which asks people to care for others altruistically, runs up against the profit motive impelling people to act selfishly. Cut and paste, pick and choose as we might, we consistently face dilemma after dilemma. We discover a world of never-ending and frustrating conflict.

Perhaps this is the way the world is supposed to be, especially within democratic government. The give and take. The checks and balances. The selfishness of the individual held in check by the higher expectations of the Church and the altruism required of family life. The obsessive-compulsive priority of making money through the corporation balanced against the broader priorities of the state. Perhaps it all works out in the end. Perhaps asking for just one center-point is not only unrealistic but unfair.

THE FAMILY UNIT

Actually, it is neither unrealistic nor unfair to demand that we settle on one fundamental unit of society. We are not asking that one path be chosen to the exclusion of all others. The reason that each organizing principle is a viable option is that each is so fully integrated into our lives. We are individuals. We do express religious faith in meaningful ways. We do enjoy work and making money. And we recognize that a modicum of order and submission is required to live safely and peaceably in community.

However, here is our claim.

Every strength of each potential organizing center is maximized through the filter of the natural family as the fundamental unit of society. The unique strengths of the individual are magnified within the context of the natural family. Religious life has greater meaning in this context. Work and earning money are given full purpose. And the state is more effective in its role when families are strong and autonomous. All of the other organizing principles become stronger when we base society on the natural family. The same cannot be said of any of the others.

All facets of life are enriched when we choose the natural family as the fundamental unit of society. Our social life is richer—we experience broad diversity within a context of stable familiarity. Our cultural life is richer—we are better able to take advantage of generational experience and the lessons of tradition. Our political life is richer—strong, autonomous families maximize the best functions of democracy. Our economic life is richer—we work with lasting purpose, cooperatively and altruistically, for others and not just for ourselves. And our spiritual life is richer—we are motivated to become our better selves as we give birth and nurturing to the rising generations.

The natural family is the key to the fullness of life. It does what no other organizing principle can do—it makes everything around it better, it amplifies the best elements of all other institutions. It is the foundation of ordered liberty.

Eternal Truths and the Sciences

THE HEART AND SOUL of *The Natural Family* are those sections telling "the story of the family" and offering "a vision" for our common future. The former looks to a new couple and narrates their life as an archetype. It follows them from the first signs of mutual attraction through marriage, homebuilding, childbirth, parenting, and the grandparent years, to their final rest. The latter section looks to culture and society, and points toward an abundant landscape of fruitful family homes, filled with productive activity and animated by the sounds of many children.

We readily admit that these portraits of the natural family appeal to ideals. They are intended to inspire, to motivate, and to encourage. We hope they fire others' imaginations, as they have fired our own. We especially hope they will turn the aspirations and the dreams of the young toward home- and family-building.

Still, we also ground this story and this vision in the natural world, where their truths are open to study and confirmation by the physical and social sciences. Being "natural" means that the family rests within the created order. It is open to honest investigation, to fair scrutiny. The natural family welcomes scientific inquiry, with the confidence of welcoming a friend.

It is true that during much of the twentieth century the opinion was widespread that social science was hostile to traditional family relations. As one analyst explained in 1917, "the new view is that the higher and more obligatory relation is to society rather than the family."[1] The Swedish economist Gunnar Myrdal also underscored the radical nature of the social sciences. There were, he insisted, no lasting economic or social laws, no "natural" institutions, for the whole of human institutional life was a variable. Moreover, Myrdal held that the scientific analysis of social problems pointed toward the use of *preventive* policies, in which the goal was to prevent social problems, not to cure them after they appeared. He said that such preventive social policy led to a "natural marriage" of the correct technical and the politically radical solution. Accordingly, Myrdal insisted that the social sciences were in fact subversive of the family and other traditional institutions.[2]

This close identification of sociology with radical politics during much of the twentieth century is based on error, on the subordination of true science to ideology. As Robert Nisbet's extraordinary work *The Sociological Imagination* reminds us, all of the great European founders of sociology were actually inspired by socially *conservative* impulses or questions. Auguste Comte, Alexis de Tocqueville, Ferdinand Tönnies, Frederic LePlay, Emile Durkheim, Max Weber, Georg Simmel, Herbert Spencer—all found inspiration, direct or indirect, from the anti-Enlightenment, so-called "reactionary" writers of nineteenth-century France, social critics such as Bonald, de Maistre, Chateaubriand. They were drawn to a new analysis of social order by the great disruptions of the industrial revolution, and by the excesses of individualism.

According to Nisbet, the very unit-ideas of sociology—analysis of family, community, tradition, authority, status, the sacred, alienation—all show "an unusually close relation" with "the principal tenets of philosophical conservatism." As Nisbet concludes, "the [creative] paradox of sociology . . . lies in the fact that although it falls, in its objectives and in the political and scientific values of its principal figures, in the mainstream of modernism, its essential concepts and its implicit perspectives place it much closer . . . to philosophical conservatism."[3]

Accordingly, we expect social science done well and true to reveal the necessary, irreplaceable position of the "natural family." And this is, we argue, the primary finding of the social sciences over the last twenty-five years. In terms of adult well-being, child well-being, and social well-being, the social sciences point to children living with their two natural, biological parents in a married couple home as the ideal setting for healthy, happy, and enriching human lives. *Any deviation* from this model—cohabitation, adoption, divorce, out-of-wedlock birth, remarriage, "same-sex marriage"—raises the probability of negative outcomes.

Let us be more specific, weaving together statements found in the manifesto with the results of scientific investigations.

The small home economy remains
the vital center of daily existence.

Although the relative size of the household sector of the American economy fell steadily from 1930 to 1985, household production in 1985 still accounted for goods and services valued at 28 percent of the value of all goods and services in the market sector of the economy. Indeed, economic analysis shows that the value of home production in 1973 exceeded 60 percent of the typical American family's money income before taxes and 70 percent of the typical American family's money income after taxes. The value of home production ran highest for families with young children. In these families, it was almost equal to the value of money income after taxes. The value of home production was affected only slightly by wives' employment. Analyses performed by economists from the University of Chicago and Stanford University reveal that "the average two-earner family requires about 30 percent more money income to achieve the same . . . standard of living as a one-earner family" because of higher expenditures for "non-durable goods and purchases of services" of the sort that the one-income family does not need because of the productivity of its own home economy. Looking at a similar nation, careful economic analysis reveals that the economic value of home production in Australia in the late twentieth century was approximately the same as that of the market production measured in the official Australian economy.[4]

*Husband and wife learn that family and
faith are, in fact, two sides of the same coin.*

A nationwide Canadian study provides strong evidence that religious faith fosters enduring marriages. Among Canadian couples who attended church services at least weekly, less than one-fifth dissolved their marriages within twenty-five years, compared to almost half of couples who attended church services seldom or never. In fact, survey research indicates that religiosity serves as a better indicator of marital strength than does family development (e.g., number of children or duration of marital union) or socioeconomic position. The researchers view these findings as clear evidence that religion is "a source of strength and vitality for relationships." In another study, investigators trace a strong pattern linking elements of religiosity to positive marital adjustment. In particular, higher levels of "ritualistic involvement," of "religious experience," and of "conservative" religious belief predict higher levels of marital consensus, satisfaction, and cohesion.[5]

Survey data also show a consistent linkage between creedal assent and active church participation on the one hand and marital success on the other. The researchers see "belief, effort, and participation in religion" as a strong predictor of "better marital adjustment, happiness and satisfaction." Taking a broader look, the prominent bioethicist Leon Kass marvels at the mystery of sexual complementarity, a mystery so deep that it offers "an opening to the truly transcendent and eternal" and inspires "awe in the face of life and sex and love and other great powers not of our making," including "the creative powers exercisable through procreative handing down of our living humanity to the next generation." Thirteen leading social scientists identify "a religious or spiritual orientation" as a component of "strong families," a defining aspect emerging in study and after study.[6]

> *The truly rich family draws on the*
> *strengths of three or more generations.*

Grandparents matter. Two pediatricians credit grandparents with giving their grandchildren a "better overall view of human growth and development" than younger teachers could do. Psychiatric evidence also suggests that "the grandparent-grandchild bond is second only in emotional significance to the parent-child bond." Other social scientists have compiled the psychological and sociological research indicating that grandparents do much to give their grandchildren a sense of emotional security and cultural continuity. The researchers stress "the symbolic, indirect, and direct influences of grandparents" on their grandchildren.[7]

Family households, formerly function-rich
beehives of useful, productive work and
mutual support, tended to become merely
functionless, overnight places of rest
for persons whose active lives and
loyalties lay elsewhere.

Historical analysis exposes as a failure the attempt to renew family life by focusing solely on the companionate husband-wife union while allowing continued erosion of the productive home economy. Though cultural enthusiasm for the companionate marriage did foster short-term renewal in family life (from about 1945 to 1960), the lack of any enduring basis for household production within this type of marriage left it vulnerable, allowing the unraveling of marriage and home life between 1965 and 1980. Thus, a conception of the family rooted in shared consumption and emotional support "failed as a meaningful focus of American loyalty and as a bulwark against both the ambitions of the state and the atomizing incentives of the economy." Analysts attribute the decline in the relative size of the household sector of the economy to the movement of wives and mothers into paid employment. Because economists have typically ignored the household sector of the economy, the shift of production from the household to the market has exaggerated real economic growth in recent decades. Cultural and economic analysis also traces the "festering contradiction of modern womanhood" to the "displacement of crafts," which denied homemakers their traditional productive role by converting them into mere consumers. Intergenerational survey evidence further indicates that young Americans are increasingly shifting their loyalties away from the family and home, toward themselves and the state.[8]

Cultural and economic histories also show how Americans, increasingly entranced by science and efficiency, came to de-value the skills of the traditional homemaker. Because of this de-valuation, more and more women became dissatisfied with a home-based social role. Karl Polanyi's classic work of economic history shows how the rise of market capitalism displaced cottage- and village-based enterprises. The self-sufficient household that satisfied most of its needs through its own home-centered labor gave way to the consumer household dependent on cash income to satisfy its needs through money purchases in the marketplace. Pitirim Sorokin also shows that the loss of the home's productive functions—a loss reducing the home to "a mere incidental parking place"—is one of the twentieth-century's most damaging developments.[9]

We affirm that the natural family
is a fixed aspect of the created order,
one ingrained in human nature.

Humankind has been conjugal since its first appearance on earth. Evolutionary anthropologists identify "the two-parent family household" as a defining characteristic of the species. Tracing the course of human evolution, these scientists highlight the importance of the "sex-based division of labor" that established itself within the "productive pair bond," so creating a "dual economy specific to hominids." It was the remarkable success of this dual economy that made possible "a social revolution . . . from a more apelike to a more human way of life." From a different discipline, a mathematical-genetic model offers an evolutionary explanation for the emergence of monogamy. This model predicts that female mating will naturally tend toward a pattern in which each female has all of her offspring with a single mate.[10]

> *We affirm that the natural family is*
> *the ideal, optimal, true family system.*

This statement drives to the core of scientific inquiry. For instance, a task force appointed by the American Academy of Pediatrics (AAP) concludes that "unequivocally, children do best when they are living with [two] mutually committed and loving parents who respect and love one another." The AAP scholars stress that children do not enjoy the same advantages in a stepfamily or in a household headed by unmarried cohabiting parents. Scrutiny of data collected in 1999 from a nationally representative sample of nearly forty thousand children (ages six to eleven) and adolescents (ages twelve to seventeen) also reveals that "those living outside of two-biological-parent married families tend to report more behavioral and emotional problems and less school engagement" than do peers living in two-biological-parent married families. The data especially indicate adverse outcomes for children living in households headed by cohabiting couples. Though the distinctively high incidence of problems among young children (ages six to eleven) in homes headed by cohabiting parents can be statistically attributed to economic circumstances, economic variables do *not* account for the high incidence of problems among *adolescents* in households headed by cohabitors.[11]

Similarly, in psychological and academic data collected from 349 young adolescents, researchers find more support for a "family structure perspective" than for any competing theoretical perspective. "For the most part," the authors of the new study remark, "children who lived with their biological parents had fewer behavior problems and better general adjustment in school than children who lived with divorced parents or with mothers who had remarried." The evidence is overwhelming: "Family structure was associated with six of seven indicators of child's adjustment," with children in intact families achieving higher grades and engaging in fewer problem behaviors than peers in single-parent or step-families.[12]

Such results appear time and again. Data from a nationally representative sample of 850 households reveals "a consistent pattern," the intact family provides the best environment for fostering adolescent well-being: "Adolescents whose mothers and fathers are both in their first marriage have the fewest problems with socio-emotional adjustment, academic performance, and global well-being." In a study of delinquency based on a nationally representative sample of more than 20,000 adolescents in grades seven through twelve, researchers at the National Institute of Child Health and Human Development found not only that teen criminality runs lowest among teens from two-biological-married-parent families, but also that levels of parental involvement, supervision, monitoring, and closeness all average highest in these families.[13]

Other researchers assess adolescent well-being in four types of family structures: those headed by married biological parents; those headed by unmarried single mothers; those headed by a biological parent married to a step-parent; and those headed by a biological parent cohabiting with a partner. Not surprisingly, the researchers conclude that "adolescents living in married, two-biological-parent families generally fare better than teenagers living in any other family type." More specifically, adolescents in intact two-parent families are less likely than peers from other family types to be suspended or expelled from school, less likely to commit delinquent crimes, less likely to be reported for problem behaviors at school, less likely to receive low grades in two or more subjects, and more likely to score well on standard tests of cognitive development.[14]

In a similar study, comparative statistical analysis shows that the nuclear family is far more stable than five other household forms—single individual, couple (no children), single parent, other family types, and other non-family types. The researchers calculate that half of the spells that people spend in the nuclear family last for seven or more years. In contrast, other non-family households were "extremely transitory," with a median survival time of less than two years and with less than a tenth of spells in such households enduring more than five years. Median survival times for non-nuclear family types, including single-parent households, were only three to four years.[15]

Given the instability of these family types, it is hardly surprising that FBI and U.S. Census Bureau numbers show that among the nation's white majority, "diversification" in family forms significantly drives up the homicide rate. The researchers speculate that "as white families become increasingly diversified from traditional forms," they are losing their "means of coping" and the "informal social control [necessary] to impede violence."[16]

Similar results emerge around the globe. Comparative ethnography indicates that "virtually all marriage systems across the world reinforce a pair-bonding template." The reason that pair-bonding appears so universally important is that any "unraveling of the pair-bonding template is aligned with a number of serious society dysfunctions" that "place the commonweal at a disadvantage" in comparison with societies based upon marriage and pair-bonding. Using data on the rate of infection with sexually transmitted diseases (STDs) to create a proxy variable indicating the frequency with which men and women move outside traditional patterns of marriage and pair-bonding, researchers have established a strong correlation between STD rates on the one hand and infant mortality, violent crime, and depressed high-school graduation rates on the other. It would appear that "a jettisoning of pair-bonding/marriage . . . reverberates throughout the community in a myriad of negative or adverse consequences."[17]

All other "family forms" are incomplete
or are fabrications of the state.

The tension between the natural family and the state is considerable. Two sociologists conclude that government policy has made children an artificial economic asset in the "mother-state-child" family, a family form that multiplies because of state subsidies. A Scandinavian analyst identifies the rise of the welfare state as the development that ended women's dependence upon men in traditional family circumstances. It is the welfare state that mediates transfer payments from men to women outside of the family. And it is the welfare state that effects "a redistribution of jobs between the sexes" by creating a "decided female bias in the public sector."[18]

The effects of state intervention are also evident to the economist Jennifer Roback Morse, who dismisses "the single-parent family" as "the mother of all myths." Some third party, she argues, is always in the background: "The person who appears to be raising a child all by herself has substituted for the other parent some combination of market-provided child care, employment income,

and government assistance." A Norwegian social scientist concludes that it was the passage of welfare state policies providing
public support for unwed mothers and their children that made
non-marital cohabitation—previously rare in Norway—a common
household arrangement. "Cohabitation as a way of life and welfare
state programs and policies accommodate . . . one another," she
writes.[19]

*The breakdown of the natural family, and moral
and political failure, not "overpopulation," account for poverty,
starvation, and environmental decay.*

The work of Nobel laureate Amartya Sen provides a framework for
showing how democratic governance serves as a protection against
famine. Despite its huge population and its vulnerability to drought
and food shortages, India has been able to avoid famine because of
its political institutions. In contrast, China and Ethiopia suffered
terrible famines not because of larger populations but because
both countries were non-democratic. *Science* magazine identifies
bad government policies—not nature or overpopulation—as the
reasons for famine in Sudan and Ethiopia. Both countries need to
overhaul national policies that retard the use of new crop strains
and to develop adequate transportation and irrigation systems.[20]

Similarly, decades of communist misrule—not overpopulation—produced "ecological devastation" in Eastern Europe and
the Soviet Union. The badly polluted air, water, and soil in these
regions drove up rates of anemia, tuberculosis, hepatitis, and other
diseases. Viewed economically, famine is "a tragic magnification of
normal market and governmental failures." Vulnerability to famine is typically the consequence of a weak national infrastructure,
government debility, and authoritarian political processes.[21]

Challenging Malthusian orthodoxy, economist Julian Simon marshals evidence that increasing human demand for food leads to technological innovation and therefore to increased agricultural production and prosperity in the broader economy. This dynamic points the analyst "in an optimistic direction with respect to humankind's ability to feed itself despite—or, more likely, because of—population growth." Large-scale economic analysis actually demonstrates that population brings "positive economic effects in the long run, though there are costs in the short run." Even when focusing on the demand for natural resources, Simon identifies technologically-mediated long-term benefits of population growth. Thus, a realistic study of population effects makes population growth a reason for optimism, not pessimism. In *The Ultimate Resource* he also argues that population growth does not necessarily hinder economic development or reduce the standard of living nor lead to environmental degradation. To the contrary, population growth tends over time to increase the standard of living for all, including ecologists. As population growth fosters technological innovation, natural resources become more and more interchangeable and scarcity turns into abundance.[22]

*We affirm that human depopulation is
the true demographic danger facing
the earth in this new century.*

Russian demographer Anatoly Antonov warns that one of the world's great nations faces "demographic failure" because of adverse trends in family life, trends he sees in other industrialized nations. Demographic disintegration and entropy are fast replacing equilibrium in Russia and other developed countries. A prominent Australian demographer views the mid-twentieth century baby

boom as no more than a "partial detour" in the long-term, economi-
cally-driven global decline in fertility. Currently depressed levels
of fertility reflect the inevitable consequences of a societal shift
from traditional "home production whether on the farm or in the
house" to modern "extra-domestic or industrial production."

Available evidence offers little support for the view that this
period of decline in family life and fertility is over. Indeed, demographers identify a looming "fertility crisis" in the industrialized
world, where completed fertility has fallen under 1.5 births per
woman in many countries, well below the 2.1 births needed just
to maintain a stable population. The "very low fertility" now being
measured in various countries (including Spain, Germany, Russia,
and Japan) portends dramatic population contraction in the years
ahead. Researchers marvel that global media outlets in the United
States, Europe, and Japan have accorded the topic "only limited
discussion." Demographers indeed wonder if perhaps "people used
to living for the here and now may have difficulty appreciating the
long-term consequences beyond their immediate horizon." Social
analyst Philip Longman warns that rapidly falling fertility rates
endanger the economic well-being and political stability of all
industrialized nations. He recommends government intervention
to create incentives for childbearing.[23]

> *Everything that a man does is mediated
> by his aptness for fatherhood. Everything
> that a woman does is mediated by her
> aptness for motherhood.*

An important thread running through fatherhood literature defines
breadwinning as "active, responsible, emotionally invested, de-
manding, expressive, and measuring real devotion." Many fathers

rank "provider" as the most important role a father can play and view providing as "a way to invest in their families." Not surprisingly, the inability to provide leads many men to withdraw from family life. A "consistent pattern" thus emerges in the paternal-involvement literature: namely, "fathers who provide are involved in many aspects of their children's lives; fathers who do not provide disengage from involvement with their children." Similarly, a medical researcher adduces evidence that mothers can, through their maternal nurturance, give their children "a protective factor" in psychological development that neither fathers nor non-parental caregivers can provide. Indeed, when it takes place within marriage, motherhood safeguards good health in ways predicted by "role enhancement" theory. The status of married motherhood thus fosters decidedly "favorable outcomes" for women who take it on.[24]

To the great surprise of the researcher involved, even students completing law and MBA degrees emphasize the primacy of their future family roles as spouses and parents when interviewed about their future hopes. Only a small subgroup of students, mostly female, anticipate creating a surrogate "family" through friendship. Elsewhere, survey data reveal that young Americans in the 1990s were much more committed to marriage and family life and regarded both motherhood and fatherhood as "more fulfilling" than did their counterparts in the 1970s. Though some elements of American culture remain in tension with traditional understandings of family life, it appears that most young Americans still view wedlock and children as "centrally significant and meaningful." Marriage and children may even have become "more valued, desired, and expected" in recent years. Historical investigation also highlights the reasons many American women responded favorably to the La Leche League's understanding of motherhood as "a valid vocation" and as a "liberating career." These women found their sense of social identity in motherhood conceived as "a rewarding job, a job filled with all sorts of satisfactions."[25]

We affirm that the complementarity of
the sexes is a source of strength.

When Nobel laureate Gary Becker applies his economic theory to family life, he demonstrates that a successful marriage benefits both the husband and the wife because of a gender complementarity that "maximizes total output because the gain from the division of labor is maximized." Bioethicist Leon Kass, whose perspective reflects both modern science and ancient scripture, marvels at the mystery of sexual complementarity. The marvelous elements of sexual relations—including explosive elements "almost guaranteed to cause trouble"—can be "clothed by culture, and altered by customs, rituals, beliefs, and diverse institutional arrangements." Yet "the elements themselves are none of them cultural constructions, nor is there likely to be any conceivable cultural arrangement that can harmonize to anyone's satisfaction all their discordant tendencies. On the contrary, political and cultural efforts to rationally solve the problem of man and woman . . . will almost certainly be harmful, even dehumanizing, to man, to woman, and especially to children, not least because such matters are so delicate and private, and their deeper meanings inexpressible."[26]

Men and women exhibit profound
biological and psychological differences.

The evidence here is vast. Survey data from thirty-seven cultures worldwide, for example, confirm the predictions of evolutionary theory about diverging male-female mate preferences. In all cultures surveyed, women value potential mates regarded as capable of acquiring resources while men value a physical attractiveness indicative of reproductive capacity. Thus, in all thirty-seven cultures, women favored potential mates who were somewhat older than they, while men favored potential mates who were somewhat younger. The monitoring of newborn infants exposed to mild stress reveals significant and consistent sex differences in both behavioral and neurochemical responses. Such sex differences, the researchers note, are clearly "prior to socialization." In fact, anatomists see a remarkable sex difference in the structure of male and female human brains. Sex differences in the splenium of the corpus callosum suggest that the female brain manifests "less hemispheric specialization" than does the male brain.[27]

A very broad and inclusive survey of empirical studies indicates that men and women differ in other significant ways as well. Many of these male-female differences are remarkably consistent and large. One prominent investigator has noted that empirical studies have not only failed to provide the evidence feminists were looking for to discredit stereotypes, they have actually "produced findings that conform to people's ideas about the sexes." Repeated studies have shown that human males consistently manifest greater aggression than human females. Another investigator has reported that men and women differ in the way they attack and solve intellectual problems. The differences reflect the way sex hormones affect brain organization. The neurological evidence thus indicates that from the very start of life "the environment is acting on differently wired brains in boys and girls."[28]

Indeed, the results for seven gender-role surveys conducted between 1974 and 1997 reveal a pattern of "stability" or even one of "increasing sex typing" over this twenty-three-year period. The researchers interpret this pattern as evidence of "predispositions based on innate patterns as posited by the evolutionary model." The differences first manifest themselves in infancy. Observation of newborn infants establishes a consistent sex difference in response to the odor of human breast milk: whereas female infants with no prior breastfeeding experience are consistently attracted to the odor of human breast milk, male infants with no prior breastfeeding experience consistently fail to manifest any such attraction. In cognitive tests administered in Japan and the United States, researchers limn an "almost identical pattern of sex differences," with males in both countries outperforming females in tests of visual-spatial skills and females in both countries outperforming males in tests of verbal ability. The researchers see in their findings a need for "biologically based" explanations of the differences.[29]

An extensive analysis of biological data for various species establishes that males and females—including human males and human females—are biologically predisposed to follow different life paths and to deploy distinctively different tactics during their individual development. In humans, major cognitive differences emerge early in fetal development and are reinforced during puberty. These biological differences affect human sexual behavior, psychology, and gender role identity. Because these biological differences are "not correlated with socialization," it is not surprising that in recent decades of cultural turmoil the evidence indicates "no consistent tendency for sex differences in social behavior and personality to have eroded." Empirical data collected from various countries actually indicate "near universality of sex differences in spatial abilities across human cultures." Evolutionary theorists interpret this pattern as evidence of a sexual division of labor during hominid evolution, as males did most of the hunting and females did most of the foraging.[30]

Surveying evidence gleaned from military and police records, a prominent social theorist concludes that even the most aggressively feminist policies have not erased "the fact that women's bodies are much less suitable [than men's] for engaging in violence or defending against [it]." Because modern technology has not eliminated the importance of this basic biological difference and because "no society can survive without either the use of violence or the threat of it, . . . complete equality between men and women will never be realized." Indeed, investigation of the biological effects of sex hormones makes it impossible to accept the view that gender roles reflect merely social conditioning and strongly indicates that "sex differences in hormone experience from gestation to adulthood shape gendered behavior." It would appear that "gendered social structure is a universal accommodation to this biological fact." One researcher has even warned that if societies "depart too far from the underlying sex-dimorphism of biological predispositions, they will generate social malaise and social pressures to drift back toward closer alignment with biology. A social engineering program to degender society would require a Maoist approach: continuous renewal of revolutionary resolve and a tolerance for conflict."[31]

When a man and a woman are united in marriage
the whole is greater than the sum of the parts.

Applying economic theory to family life, Becker shows that love in a marriage "raises commodity output" and that caring in a marriage raises the couple's "total income" by making part of their output a "family commodity." Government economic data indicates that once men take on the role of breadwinner—a role traditionally defined as complementary to the wife's homemaker role—they become more productive. That is, "marriage *per se* makes [male] workers more productive."[32]

Ideas and religious faith can prevail
over material forces. Even one as
powerful as industrialization can be
tamed by the exercise of human will.

Around the globe, we find encouragement here. Survey data show that during the same years (1982 to 1988) that the overall percentage of eighteen-year-old white American females who were virgins fell from 51 percent to 42 percent, the percentage of eighteen-year-old white fundamentalist Protestants who were virgins actually rose from 45 percent to 61 percent. An economic analysis of the social dynamics that obtain in the secular state of Sweden reveals that the presence of church-attending men and women in a Swedish neighborhood significantly reduces rates of abortion, divorce, bankruptcy, and out-of-wedlock births, even among the non-believers who live in these neighborhoods. A team of pediatric researchers identify religion as a primary reason for the remarkably low levels of sexual activity among Hispanic young women: almost 60 percent of the unmarried women surveyed in this study were still virgins, compared to 35 to 50 percent for the general American population.[33]

We will end state incentives
to live outside of marriage.

This deplorable situation is well documented. Two sociologists conclude that government welfare policies make married fatherhood particularly burdensome because married fathers must support their own children directly and other men's children indirectly—through taxes paid to cover the cost of the welfare system. Census and vital statistics data for 1980 indicate that the level of public assistance available was "strongly related to African-American family structure" in urban areas, with higher levels of assistance pushing down rates for marriage and marital fertility and reducing the percentage of children residing in husband-wife families.[34]

In data from a nationally representative sample of 6,288 young women between the ages of fourteen and twenty-two, researchers identify evidence that "higher average welfare payments depressed marriage rates among poor women." The analysis suggests that "poor women may have lower rates of first marriage because the availability [of welfare benefits] is perceived as an economically viable potential alternative to marrying an unacceptable mate, especially in the event of nonmarital child-bearing." The researchers add that "the generosity of public assistance may enter women's calculations of the relative benefits of marriage versus singlehood, regardless of whether public assistance is actually received."[35]

Policy analysis suggests that small reductions in welfare translate into small reductions in illegitimacy but that complete abolition of welfare would produce dramatic reduction in illegitimacy. Between 1940 and 1990, the growth of the entire welfare package (not just Aid to Families with Dependent Children but Medicaid, food stamps, and housing subsidies) dramatically parallels the rise in illegitimacy among blacks. One analyst has shown how the welfare-to-work elements of welfare reform have created a mixed combination of incentives and disincentives to marry. Though there is as yet "little evidence of large effects," the Earned Income Tax Credit in particular creates a significant disincentive for employed unwed mothers to marry. Sociological and economic analyses of recent welfare reforms indicates that the termination of Aid to Families with Dependent Children (AFDC) has been accompanied by a decline in out-of-wedlock childbearing, a leveling off or slight reduction in the divorce rate, and a modest reduction in the number of female-headed households.[36]

We will end state preferences for easy
divorce by repealing "no-fault" statutes.

The "no-fault" revolution independently damaged marriage. Economist Douglas Allen challenges statistical methods used to demonstrate that adoption of no-fault laws had no net effect on divorce rates. More reliable statistical methods suggest that adoption of such laws pushed the divorce rate higher. Indeed, statistical analysis of historical data establishes that 17 percent of the rise in the U.S. divorce rate between 1968 and 1988 can be attributed to adoption of new laws permitting unilateral divorce. Another study using data from thirty-eight states yields strong evidence that adoption of no-fault drove up the divorce rate in eight of them (including California) and lesser evidence that it drove up the divorce rate in eight more (including New York). In these sixteen states, the adoption of no-fault statutes appears to have increased the divorce rate by 20 to 25 percent.[37]

Scholars at the University of Oklahoma provide statistical evidence that the adoption of no-fault clearly drove up the divorce rate in forty-four of the fifty states, the six exceptions "being directly interpretable because of peculiarities." The overall statistical pattern indicates that adoption of no-fault had "a large effect" on divorce rates.[38]

Family law specialist Lynn Wardle criticizes no-fault not only for its unintended consequences (such as the impoverishment of women) but also for its failure to fulfill the declared intentions of its advocates. While proponents of no-fault promised that its passage would reduce adversarial litigation, Wardle finds that any reduction in hostile litigation over the grounds for divorce has been achieved merely by a "transfer of hostility into other facets of the divorce proceeding rather than [through] any substantial reduction in the acrimony of the proceeding overall." In fact, the enactment of no-fault statutes has "exacerbated the trauma of divorce" for many children and struggling parents, while the legal profession itself has emerged as "the major beneficiary of the no-fault divorce reforms." Lenore J. Weitzman concludes that as a radical change in the way marriage ends, no-fault divorce inevitably "affects the rules for marriage itself and the intentions and expectations of those who enter it." No-fault divorce thus "redefines marriage as a time-limited, contingent arrangement rather than a lifelong commitment."[39]

— 5 —

Life, Death, Work, and Taxes

EMPIRICAL RESEARCH reveals the importance of the natural family as we consider questions of health, wealth creation, sexual identity, education, faith, and even taxes. As in the previous chapter, we draw on the lessons of science to affirm the ideals articulated in the manifesto.

We will allow private insurers to recognize
the health advantages of marriage and family living,
according to sound business principles.

Family living delivers improved health, an old actuarial truth. A legal analyst identifies group risk assessment as a type of classification "at the heart of the insurance system." Noting that in a market-based system, insurers have "a strong incentive" to assess group risk accurately, he concludes that insurance classification fosters economically efficient behavior. It is assessment of group risk that explains why life insurance premiums differ for men and women and for smokers and non-smokers. It is assessment of group risk that also explains why auto insurance companies often consider marital status in setting premiums. Indeed, analysis of the pronounced health and mortality advantage that married men and women enjoy over unmarried peers provides a solid risk-exposure rationale for "restructuring Medicare rates so that married recipients pay a lower monthly premium than the unmarried." Since many Americans remain unmarried because of circumstances beyond their control, actual enactment of such a restructuring is politically doubtful and ethically questionable and therefore compels consideration of other political options (such as tax credits helping young married couples with children) for rewarding family behavior that reduces medical costs. Though this analysis does not look at policies for private health and life insurers, it offers a complete justification for such insurers (who operate outside the constraints on public policymakers and who already offer lower life-insurance premiums to women than to men and lower life- and health-insurance premiums to non-smokers than to smokers) to offer premium reductions to married policy holders.[1]

Confirmation of this link between good health and family living can be found globally. For example, survey data for Dutch adults indicate that married men and women enjoy better health than single, divorced, or cohabiting peers. Although positive health habits account for some of married adults' health advantage, more than half of that advantage persists in statistical models that take such habits into account. Researchers theorize that differences in psychological or material circumstances may account for the rest of married couples' distinct advantage in health.[2]

Ohio State medical researchers report finding significantly lower levels of immunizing antibodies in blood samples drawn from divorced and separated individuals than in blood samples

drawn from married peers. The impairment of their immune systems leaves divorced and separated individuals more vulnerable to
certain physical ailments (including pneumonia and tuberculosis)
than are their married counterparts. Two national health surveys
conducted in France indicate that married mothers with children
at home enjoy the kind of health improvement predicted by "role
enhancement" theory. In contrast, single mothers suffer from "very
unfavorable outcomes in terms of perceived health and malaise
symptoms."[3]

Princeton scholars have examined data from twenty-six
developed nations (from Austria to New Zealand and Singapore)
to understand the relationship between marital status and mortality.
In all of them, "married persons of both sexes experience a marked
mortality advantage relative to single individuals." The fact that
sickly men and women usually do not marry accounts for only a
small portion of the married-single differential in mortality rates.
Health records for a national sample of young women indicate
that "women who were not married generally had worse health
trends than married women." To the researchers' acknowledged
surprise, "the health effects of being never married were as harmful or somewhat more harmful than the health effects of being
divorced or separated."[4]

We will end the oppressive taxation of
family income, labor, property, and wealth.

Tax policy can have a profound effect on family health. Historically rooted analysis justifies tax preferences for married couples
and tax penalties for divorce and non-marital cohabitation. Because the pro-family tax principles on which American tax policy

was erected in the post-war era were ignored and even attacked by policymakers in the 1960s and 1970s, government increasingly fostered childlessness and divorce. The Tax Reform Act of 1986 only partly remedied the tax bias against married couples with children, particularly one-income married couples. Analysis in 1987 of historical tax patterns highlights how families were hurt between 1960 and 1985 by the remarkable erosion of the value of the personal exemption allowed for by the Federal income tax code. Because of this erosion, the fraction of median income exempt from taxation fell for the average four-person family from more than three-fourths in 1948 to less than one-third in 1983. By raising the value of the personal exemption to $2400 (more than double its 1986 value of $1080), the 1986 tax reform partially remedied this erosion; however, giving the exemption the same relative value that it had in 1948 (measured as a fraction of per capita income) would have meant raising it to approximately $5,600. A Treasury Department analyst identifies this erosion as, "by almost any measure. . . . the largest single change in the income tax in the postwar era." This erosion particularly hurt families with children.[5]

The estate tax is also anti-family. Those who support confiscatory estate taxes on the basis of progressive social theories are ignoring the way such taxes deplete capital accrual by creating disincentives to work and save. Through the estate tax, in fact, government is "'punishing' the Thrifty clan vis-à-vis Spendthrift." The estate tax thus works as "the opposite of a sin tax" and may actually be "a virtue tax" because it "penalizes people who get wealth and then save it for their children." The property tax likewise acts as "a virtue tax." Economic analysis demonstrates that under almost any set of statistical assumptions, a tax on housing property is "regressive" toward the lower- to middle-income segments of the population. Congressional hearings in 2001 began with an acknowledgment of the "growing consensus that we must provide income-tax relief for married couples." Testimony during the hearing did show how the Bush Administration provided some relief, chiefly by increasing the size of the personal income tax exemption. However, expert testimony also highlighted the failure to help moderate-income couples not eligible for the child tax benefits available to unmarried peers, a failure that creates "very high marriage penalties." Analysis further showed that attempts to reform the Earned Income Tax Credit (EITC) had "not come close to eliminating EITC marriage penalties."[6]

> *We will end taxes, financial incentives,*
> *subsidies, and zoning laws that discourage*
> *small farms and family-held businesses.*

Historical investigation identifies current legal pressures against home-based handicraft work as the legacy of the New Deal crusade against sweatshop-style industrial homework. Though investigator Eileen Boris acknowledges the risk of abuse, she recognizes the powerful appeal of home-based labor as "a merger of home life [and work] that promises unity in a fragmented world." Similarly, because tax policy for farmland encourages absentee ownership, it has helped drive down the number of farmers who are owner-operators. Tax policy has also encouraged farmers to incorporate their farm in order to reduce their tax burden and then to expand after incorporation. Tax policy thus denies benefits to small, unincorporated family farms that are granted to large, incorporated farms. Tax policy has also created various "problems that are unrelated to traditional farm production," problems that can frequently be resolved only with sophisticated tax advice from specialists.[7]

International social analysis identifies the ways in which family businesses benefit society in ways that other businesses cannot. Because those who run family businesses seek more than merely financial profit, they can humanize a free-market economy. Society has consequently suffered as a result of recent adverse pressures driving many family businesses to insolvency. On the other hand, society has benefited through the growth of telecommuting and other technologies favoring at-home labor. Although U.S. census data does show that white-collar home-based workers earn less than their conventional office-based counterparts, researchers adduce evidence that "argues against exploitation" as the reason for this gap. Rather, it appears that home-based workers are willing to work for less because they seek an equilibrium between income needs and family-schedule flexibility.[8]

It is not equilibrium but disruption, however, one researcher highlights when examining state "relocation subsidies" frequently available to large corporations moving into a new community, subsidies unmatched by any subsidies for the smaller family businesses in the area even though these family enterprises are often economically threatened by the corporate move-in. Meanwhile, a high-profile lawsuit highlights claims by small businesses that inducements granted by federal, state, and local governments to DaimlerChrylser to stay in Ohio force them to subsidize the huge corporation. No small family-held business ever receives such inducements.[9]

We will end the aggressive
state promotion of androgyny.

The evidence is overwhelming: androgyny—the negation of male and female—is a political creation, an act of war against human nature. Fourteen years of survey data from undergraduate college students contradicts "speculation" about widespread movement toward gender androgyny. Data indicate that the measurable psychological difference between the sexes has "not decreased over a whole generation of American life." "It is," psychologist Robert Baldwin suggests, "the concept of androgyny which should be called into question." Historical investigation exposes fraud, distortion, and deception in media and government efforts to deny male-female differences. Analysis shows that such efforts derive from ideology, not honest science. Psychologist Alice Eagley sees "a powerful political agenda" at work trying to marginalize, distort, deny, and suppress research documenting important and sizable differences between men and women. Investigation of the biological effects of sex hormones makes it impossible to accept the view that gender roles reflect merely social conditioning and strongly indicates that "sex differences in hormone experience from gestation to adulthood shape gendered behavior." It would appear that "gendered social structure is a universal accommodation to this biological fact."[10]

And yet the campaign to crush sex differences continues. Professional literature for teachers encourages them to socialize children so as to create "an androgynous society" in which there are "no stereotypical behavioral differences between males and females based solely on sex." Teachers are warned about how "adults can box children into stereotypical roles at a very young age" and are therefore guided toward children's books needed for a "non-sexist education." One federally-published guide explicitly stresses "the concept of androgyny" as the key to "a fresh look at sex roles" that will lead to "challenging gender norms." Educators are told to involve children in "reverse-role playing" in family circumstances. And because "free play, after all, means sexist play," educators are to restrict such free play and intervene in it to eliminate the traditional gender roles it might reflect. This guide also informs educators that the campaign against traditional gender roles must be "pervasive in the school setting." Educators must regard parents as a problem if they "undercut" the campaign against traditional gender roles. Educators should work towards a world in which traditional gender roles are "eliminated."[11]

We will end laws that prohibit employers from recognizing and rewarding family responsibility.

Statistical analysis shows that the "family wage economy"—created by labor leaders and progressives to support family life by enabling a male wage-earner to support a wife and children—proved remarkably stable until the mid-1970s, when the United States began to move rapidly toward "an economy of pure gender equality." Since family life has eroded in the new economic circumstances and since the assumptions on which the old family-wage economy was erected are no longer politically sustainable, one analyst proposes a package of family-based tax breaks that would deliver many of the same benefits as the old family-wage system.[12]

Economic analysis further suggests that rising numbers of young mothers have moved into paid employment because men's wages have stagnated since the 1970s, so creating "economic uncertainty and fear of downward mobility." Indeed, it was precisely "when husbands' wages began to drop [that] young mothers' employment rates increased." But the movement of young mothers into paid employment has created a "work-family dilemma" for families with young children. One researcher sees an "absence of a work-family dilemma" in past decades when Americans saw "husbands earning a family wage."[13]

Historical analysis helps identify one reason for the erosion of the family wage by exposing the way that a dubious alignment of Dixiecrat segregationists and equity feminists added a prohibition against sex discrimination to the Civil Rights Act of 1964. The Dixiecrats, it appears, hoped to kill the entire measure through this change; instead, they damaged the family. This legal change dramatically undermined the family-wage system that labor leaders and progressive maternalists had created to enable a wage-earning father to support his wife and children. The consequences were a higher divorce rate and a lower marriage rate.[14]

> *We will end discriminatory taxes and policies*
> *that favor mass state education of the young.*

Monopolies produce poor results, especially in education. Though wary of policies that would give public money to private schools, an educational analyst finds ample evidence of the need to "break up the complacent consumer-insensitive monopoly relationship that public schools enjoy in relationship to most of their clients." He also acknowledges that, under policies denying parents the option of taking children out of the public schools, parental liberty is "inhibited." An economist provides evidence suggesting that parents might well find better schools for their children in an educational system in which private contractors compete against each other than in the current system in which public schools enjoy a local monopoly. The researcher acknowledges the possibilities for abuse and fraud in a voucher system but cites notable instances of waste and malfeasance in the current order. In any case, parents with free choice in the use of vouchers might well serve as "more effective monitors [of schools' actions] than parents who have no means of rewarding or punishing the [monopoly] schools that serve their children."

Another economist takes the public schools as an example of the economic harms attendant to a monopoly. Relative to private-school teachers, public-school teachers are in the same position as a state-subsidized merchant in unfair competition with merchants receiving no such subsidy. As monopolies, public schools tend to "crowd out" private-school competitors. Consequently, "the market in education has virtually been destroyed," and a large fraction of the money spent in the U.S. on education is "social loss from monopoly."[15]

We will end abuse of "child-abuse" laws.

The campaign to end child abuse too often abuses families. One of the legal authorities who initially led the national campaign against child abuse, Douglas Besharov, presents evidence that child abuse laws are now too vague, too broad, and too easily turned against innocent parents. Coercive state intervention, he argues, should be based on "what parents did, not on what they 'might' do." Specialists in family law and child psychology at Yale University and the Hampstead Child-Therapy Clinic also warn that because even "temporary infringement of parental autonomy" weakens children's trust in their parents and increases their anxiety, state authorities ought "to err on the side of nonintrusiveness" when dealing with cases of alleged abuse.[16]

A legal expert on children's rights finds that too many children are being placed in foster care and too many parents are losing their parental rights because of child-protection systems distorted by "a bias toward over-reporting and over-labeling [of] child abuse and neglect." Because of a "pernicious shift" in public debate, "child protection" now often depends on "the virtue of breaking up families" and advocates of such protection frequently rely on rhetoric suffused with "the connotation that 'pro-parent' is 'anti-child.'" Indeed, analysis of current court proceedings in child abuse cases suggests disturbing parallels with the Salem witch trials of the seventeenth century. In many child-abuse cases, judges are shirking their duty "to distinguish between false and true accusations," as they—like their predecessors in Salem—allow misguided children to reinforce their own "prejudged certainty" of the guilt of the accused.[17]

Children are especially likely to be scripted into modern witch-trial dramas when embittered divorcing parents deploy "sex-molestation charges as a strategy to obtain custody and to achieve revenge against former spouses." A medical expert on child abuse concludes as well that "the permissive reporting aspects of the child abuse legislation" have opened the door to numerous false allegations of abuse, many lodged by "emotionally or mentally disturbed individuals." It is hardly surprising, then, that a California grand jury concludes that a disturbing number of children were being separated from their parents for extended periods because state officials were "determined to err on the side of assuming guilt" and were, consequently, "accept[ing] reports of molest[ation] as true notwithstanding that they may [have been] inherently incredible, made for motives of harm or gain, or the product of years of 'therapy.'" The grand jury calls for a higher standard of evidence in child abuse cases and for a restitution of the traditional presumption of the innocence of the accused.[18]

Human beings are made to be conjugal,
to live in homes with vital connections
to parents, spouse, and children.

The whole of human history, and pre-history, points to the family in its home as normative. Evolutionary theorists interpret the family as a unit that fits naturally within complex human patterns of human exchange and reciprocity, as a unit essential in providing "intragroup solidarity in the context of intergroup competition," and as a social group that allows post-menopausal women to serve as "post-reproductive helpers." A biologically rooted perspective on history suggests that monogamy originated as a consequence of reproductive strategies (called κ-strategies in neo-Darwinian theory) in which parents have few children but invest a great deal of care in these few. Such strategies made monogamy a necessity in the circumstances in which early humans lived, circumstances where "the cooperation of one male and one female [was] required to exploit and defend the resources." This perspective suggests that "human beings probably were never sexually promiscuous."[19]

Though polygyny has often emerged in environments in which rich and powerful men could claim more than one wife, monogamy has over time manifest "competitive advantages" by sustaining agrarian cultures dependent upon family labor and by exerting "a pacifying and stabilizing influence" on males. Interpreting ethnographic patterns in the light of the sociobiological theory of altruism, one anthropologist argues that "the emergence of monogamy in the great majority of human populations" reflects a biologically-scripted genetic logic. That same logic binds together the conjugal pair and their children in a natural unit and discourages promiscuity and adultery. In assessing the harmful effects of a communal child-rearing arrangement in which infant children slept out of the home, psychologists conclude that that the practice was harmful because it was not in harmony with the nature of the human species. The practice of moving infants out of the home and out of maternal care in this way inevitably entails deleterious consequences because it "significantly deviates from the environment of evolutionary adaptedness."[20]

We see that the family model of the 1950s was largely confined to the white majority. Black families actually showed mounting stress in these years.

The family system crafted in America during the 1950s showed surface strength—and serious shortcomings. In a landmark study, sociologist E. Franklin Frazier identifies high levels of family disruption among African-Americans who had migrated to large cities in the early twentieth century, in part because the traditional black churches had lost much of their cultural force as a consequence of the migration. Daniel Patrick Moynihan famously documented the erosion of family life within the African American community, an alarming pattern of family disintegration, and warned of the consequent "tangle of pathology." Moynihan's perception that family decay had "begun to feed on itself" within the African American community was much attacked at the time but is now widely regarded as prescient. Sociologist Charles Murray suggests that during the 1940s and 1950s the growth of welfare benefits for unwed mothers was already being paralleled by a sharp rise in black illegitimacy rates.[21]

The "companionship marriage" ideal of the 1950s,
which embraced psychological tasks to the exclusion
of material and religious functions, was fragile.

The "1950s family model" rested on a frail set of assumptions. Historical analysis exposes as an ultimate failure the attempt to renew family life by focusing solely on the companionate husband-wife union while allowing continued erosion of the productive home economy. Family sociologist Andrew Cherlin locates the shift from institutional marriage to companionate marriage within a broader cultural deinstitutionalization of wedlock. For many Americans, the companionate form of marriage has now given way to "individualized marriage," premised on maximal personal choice and individual development. The newer forms of marriage have proven less durable and more vulnerable to divorce than the traditional form of institutional marriage. Researchers have clarified the reasons for the fragility of companionate marriages focused on mutual communication and spousal support. In post-divorce interviews, men assessed the reasons they had failed in their efforts to build a companionate marriage. Repeatedly, these divorced men identified fundamental gender differences in communication styles as a reason for the marital ruptures. Former wives had tended to be more open and expressive than the men interviewed and had hoped for a communicative reciprocity that did not develop.[22]

The effort to eliminate real differences
between men and women does as much violence
to human nature and human rights as the efforts
by the communists to create "Soviet man" and
by the Nazis to create "Aryan man."

Androgyny demands and deploys an attack on human nature. Historians Becky Glass and Margaret Stolee trace disturbing parallels between the radical family policies of the Bolshevik revolutionaries who created the Soviet Union and the legislative agenda of progressive activists prominent in late-twentieth-century Western democracies. The family policies of the Bolsheviks fostered such intense "social and internal confusion" that Soviet leaders eventually abandoned them. Yet Western elites continue to press for policies that undermine "traditional and stereotypical sex roles for husbands and wives" in the same way that Bolshevik policies did.[23]

We find views against adultery and divorce
in the other great world faiths.

Scholars of religion note that in Islam divorce is regarded as "permissible but reprehensible" and that in Hinduism "marriage is treated as a sacrament and divorce is not allowed." Though Judaism and Buddhism differ remarkably in spiritual orientation and social organization, Hebrew law and Buddhist law (*miswah* and *sila*) contain notably similar moral precepts, including "universal injunctions against adultery." The appendix to C.S. Lewis' *The Abolition of Man* underscores the essential moral unity on this question.[24]

Moreover, we find recognition of the natural
family in the marriage rituals of animists.

In the six ethnic groups that constitute Vietnam's Hanhi-Lolo linguistic group, animism (in several versions) informs the religious attitudes of patriarchal clans in which marriage forges links regarded as important in this world and the next: parents-in-law are important objects of devotion in the ancestor cult. The animism of traditional Taiwanese folk religion has likewise helped to nurture "deep-rooted ideals" that make marriage "a central event in the life course." Among the many rural Taiwanese adherents to this animist tradition, "the continuity of family lineage" is imperative, and co-residence of parents with a married son persists as a common household arrangement.[25]

> *The record is clear from decades of work*
> *in sociology, psychology, anthropology,*
> *sociobiology, medicine, and social history:*
> *children do best when they are born into*
> *and raised by their two natural parents.*

This truth is unassailable. "Marriage," an American Academy of Pediatrics (AAP) task force explains, "is beneficial in many ways," in large part because "people behave differently when they are married. They have healthier lifestyles, eat better, and mother each other's health." The AAP scholars stress that children do not enjoy the same advantages in a stepfamily or in a household headed by unmarried cohabiting parents. In surveys conducted among Houston-area adolescents between 1971 and 1997, teens who had grown up in intact families were much more likely to indicate that they had received "good parenting" than were peers from single-parent or step-parent families. Having grown up in an intact family also was predictive of less psychological distress, better interpersonal relations with others, and more active social participation. Arguing against the view that genetics matters more than family structure in determining children's mental health and well-being, sociologist Andrew Cherlin cites evidence from study of female twin-pairs showing that a "parental separation or divorce increased the risk of major depression for members of a twin-pair by 42 percent, even after making allowances for genetic relatedness." This and other evidence clearly indicate that "divorce indeed has an effect on mental health . . . the variation is not due only to genes."[26]

Survey after survey indicate that children do best in intact families. Researchers find a clear pattern in the behavioral and achievements data for 12,702 young adolescents in Prince George's County near Washington, DC: "Students living with both biological parents changed more positively [during the course of the study period] than did other students." In sophisticated multivariable statistical models, an intact-family structure was consistently predictive of positive changes in the researchers' composite Success Index. Not only did an intact family predict individual success, but it also predicted the overall health of the school-neighborhood-friendship-family context in which young people live. What the researchers call high "joint context quality" exists in the network of school-neighborhood-friendship-family relationships, suggesting that intact families are essential for creating a "social world [that] is ordered in ways that generally favor young persons."

In a study of delinquency based on a nationally representative sample of more than twenty thousand adolescents in grades seven through twelve, researchers at the National Institute of Child Health and Human Development found not only that teen criminality runs lowest among teens from two-biological-married-parent families, but also that levels of parental involvement, supervision, monitoring, and closeness all average highest in these families. Northwestern scholars conclude that young men and women from single-parent and step-parent families significantly fall short of the educational attainments and occupational status typical of peers reared in intact families. The researchers trace the depressed levels of educational and occupational accomplishment found among young adults from intact families to the low levels of violence they experienced during adolescence. Indeed, the violence often experienced by teens from broken homes forms the first link in "a chain of adversity" in which "victimization undermines academic performance, educational attainment, labor force participation, occupational status, and earnings in early adulthood."[27]

Under any other setting—including one-parent . . .

The one-parent household portends large risks for children. After surveying available data, a task force appointed by the AAP expressed deep concern about social trends putting more than one-fourth of all children (26 percent) in homes headed by a single parent, usually the mother. The AAP task force points out that single-parent households have three to five times higher rates of poverty than do two-parent households and that "family income is strongly related to children's health." Moreover, "paternal absence" is predictive of "multiple and sometimes lifelong disadvantages" that go far beyond "health problems" to include "problems with school attendance, achievement and completion; emotional and behavioral problems; adolescent parenthood; substance abuse; and other risk behaviors."[28]

Studies of twins underscore this AAP finding. Data collected for 1,887 pairs of female twins born between 1975 and 1987 provide strong evidence that paternal absence increases the risk of Separation Anxiety Disorder (SAD) for young women. Statistical analysis identifies paternal absence as "an important predictor of all categories of SAD, even after accounting for other risk factors," including socioeconomic disadvantage. As a "rather robust" statistical predictor of SAD, "the loss or the threat of loss of a father figure has important consequences" in the opinion of the researchers, who note that young women suffering from SAD often manifest "impairment in functioning" at home, at school, and in relationships with peers.[29]

The effects of living in single-parent homes are particularly large for adolescents. Nationally representative data indicate that, compared to peers in intact families, teens from mother-only homes suffer from poorer socioemotional adjustment, achieve less in school, and report less favorable global well-being. The researchers identify teens in households headed by continuously-single mothers as "singularly disadvantaged" in their household resources. When researchers at the National Institute of Child Health and Human Development examine delinquency data collected from a nationally representative sample of more than twenty thousand adolescents, they identified family structure as a key predictor of teen criminality: "Adolescents in single-father families report the highest levels of delinquency, followed by those in father-step-mother and single-mother families. Delinquency levels are lowest among adolescents residing with two biological, married parents." The linkage between family structure and teen delinquency persists in a statistical model that takes into account the characteristics of the children (age, ethnicity, gender) and of the parents (education, income, immigrant status).[30]

Researchers identify father absence as a key predictor of early puberty for girls. In data collected from 281 girls participating in the Child Development Project, analysts discern evidence that "girls who were in single-mother homes at age five tended to experience earlier puberty." And unfortunately, "early onset of puberty in girls is associated with negative health and psychosocial outcomes," including "more emotional problems, such as depression and anxiety" and "alcohol consumption and sexual promiscuity."[31]

Surveying data collected from 485 youth surveyed as part of the Iowa Youth Families Projects, researchers identify "a significant increase in health problems . . . during the transition from adolescence to early adulthood" among children reared in single-parent households. "When only one parent is available in the home," the researchers remark, "the adolescent is more likely to experience conduct problems, school failures, a precocious entry into family responsibilities, a more limited education, and early stresses and strains in their work life. This accumulating process of disadvantage produces a consequent increase in risk for poor health." The researchers interpret their findings in light of previous research demonstrating that "social disadvantage in the family of origin contributes to adverse child-rearing practices of parents and in turn partially determines child adjustment problems."[32]

The effects of living in broken homes show up among young adults as well. Examining survey data collected between 1979 and 1994 for 2,846 young men tracked from ages fourteen to thirty, researchers conclude that "youth incarceration risks . . . were elevated for adolescents in father-absent households." Even after controling for household income, for the receipt of child-support payments, and for residential moves, the researchers find that "youths in father-absent families (mother-only, mother-stepfather, and relatives/other) still had significantly higher odds of incarceration than those from mother-father families." Thus, even after statistically accounting for poverty and residential moves, researchers find that sons in mother-only families were nearly twice as likely to be incarcerated as peers from mother-father families. In the simplest statistical model, researchers find that boys who are fatherless from birth are three times as likely to go to jail as peers from intact families. Similarly, in data collected from 10,353 young men and women monitored from ages seven to twenty-three, a

British-American team of researchers find evidence that young people who have experienced a parental divorce during childhood show more emotional problems, achieve less in school, and find themselves in poorer financial circumstances than do peers whose parents remain married. The researchers conclude that parental divorce often puts children of both sexes into "negative life trajectories through adolescence into adulthood."[33]

Younger children also pay a price when parents do not marry or stay married. Analyzing data collected from thirty custodial divorced mothers, thirty custodial divorced fathers, and thirty married parents with children ages six to ten, researchers found—as they expected—significantly higher levels of conduct problems among the children of divorced parents than among peers in intact families. Although the statistical model attributes much of the adverse effects of divorce to the economic and psychological hardships marital breakdown produces, none of these "intervening variables" can fully account for the statistical linkage between family structure and children's problem behaviors. Consequently, the researchers "reluctantly acknowledge" that their findings indicate that "children fare better in married, nuclear families," though they worry that such "provocative" findings are liable to "misuse by advocates of so-called 'family values.'"[34]

In nationally representative data collected from 9,398 Canadian children ages six to eleven, researchers discern a clear pattern: "children from single-mother families are at increased risk of difficulties," evident in psychiatric problems, social impairment, and depressed academic performance. Although the researchers insist (perhaps for reasons of political expediency) that "children from single-mother families develop difficulties for the same reasons as children from two-parent families," these reasons show up "at higher rates among single-mother families"—significantly higher rates. Furthermore, the evidence indicates that while "punitive parenting" sometimes causes social impairment and psychiatric problems among children in intact families, "the presence of hostile parenting in single-parent families is linked with increased psychiatric and social difficulties beyond that in two-parent families." And in broader analysis, "single-mother status on its own has a significant association with all [negative] child outcomes examined." Nationally representative social and academic data for 20,330 students likewise indicate that children from single-parent and step-parent families do significantly worse in mathematics than do peers from intact families.[35]

Poverty is another consequence of family breakdown. Economic analysis of the 1990s shows that during that decade the combined effects of a strong economy and of ever-more-aggressive government efforts to collect child support reduced the poverty rate of households with children by a mere percentage point (from 20 percent to 19 percent). The researcher identifies an increasing number of single-parent families as the reason for the stubbornly high rate for child poverty: whereas only 20 percent of children under eighteen lived in single-parent families in 1980, 25 percent did in 1990, and 28 percent in 1997. As of that latter year, nearly half of female-headed households had incomes that put them in the lowest quintile, compared to only 13 percent of married couples. More than a third of female-headed households were living below the official poverty line in 1997. The researcher warns that, compared to peers living in more favorable circumstances, "Children reared in poverty have poorer physical and mental health, do worse in school, experience more punitive discipline styles and abuse, live in poorer neighborhoods, and are more likely to engage in deviant or delinquent acts." Economic and medical data indicate that the upsurge in the number of single-parent, female-headed households has pushed an alarming number of children into both poverty and ill health. The poverty that is associated with "the loss of the wage-earning power of the absent parent, usually the father," predicts "higher rates of poor health and chronic health conditions in children," resulting in higher hospitalization and mortality rates among affected children.[36]

. . . step-parent, . . .

Unfortunately, even remarriage does little to alleviate the negative effects of family disintegration on children. After surveying available data, a task force appointed by the America Academy of Pediatrics (AAP) expressed concern about the consequences of the remarriage of a divorced parent. For although such remarriage usually improves household income, "it does not necessarily improve the experience for the child. . . . [I]n general, children who are raised in a stepfamily do about as well as do children of single mothers." An international team of social scientists finds statistical evidence that stepfather presence accelerates pubertal maturation in young girls living apart from their biological fathers. Early female puberty creates concern because it is predictive of "more emotional problems such as depression and anxiety, and. . . more problem behaviors such as alcohol consumption and sexual promiscuity." In psychological and behavioral data from a sample of eighty high schools across the country, researchers see a strong correlation between family structure and adolescents' psychological distress. "Anger," report the researchers, "is . . . more common among youth who come from blended and single-parent families compared to two-biological-parent intact families." Predictably, the researchers also find that "youth in blended and single-parent families are more delinquent than youth in two-parent biological families." In the longer term, the researchers discern a pathological pattern in which "males [laden with the kind of anger often fostered by growing up in a blended or single-parent family] in particular tend to move through a sequence of adaptations, [and] from anger to delinquency to drinking problems."[37]

Parental divorce followed by remarriage has negative educational effects as well. Comparative data provide no support for the widespread belief that remarriage improves the academic performance of children of divorced parents. These data, in fact, indicate that "remarriage following divorce has somewhat of a negative impact on the academic achievement of teenage children," with children in stepfamilies scoring significantly lower on standardized test than peers in intact families *and* in single-parent families, the comparative deficiencies being especially large in math and social studies. Indeed, the evidence indicates that *both* parental divorce *and* parental remarriage bring down children's standardized test results. Noting the general reliability of academic achievement as an indication of a child's overall emotional security and mental outlook, the researcher suggests that "remarriage adversely affects a child's psychological well-being and happiness."[38]

. . . *homosexual,* . . .

The homosexual household puts children at risk. In data gleaned from fifty-two narratives from homosexually-parented children and from forty appeals court cases involving custody disputes between homosexual and heterosexual parents, researchers adduce evidence that children reared by homosexual parents face special difficulties. Among the homosexually-reared children in the fifty-two narratives, 92 percent identified one or more problems with or concerns about the nature of their upbringing. What is more, out of 213 "score problems" in the narratives, 201 (91 percent) were "attributed to the homosexual parent(s)." And in the appellate cases surveyed, 97 percent of the harms were attributed to the homosexual parent by the courts.[39]

Lynn Wardle skeptically critiques the methodology and motives behind sociological research that puts homosexual parenting in a favorable light. He finds evidence that compared to peers reared by heterosexual parents, the children in homosexual households face a disproportionate risk of being sexually molested, of experiencing gender confusion, of becoming sexually promiscuous, of losing a parent through parental separation or death, of sliding into depression, of becoming users of illegal drugs, and of committing suicide.[40]

. . . cohabiting . . .

Cohabitation endangers children. In nationally representative data, children (ages four to sixteen) living with parents who had never married scored significantly higher on a global index of deviant behavior than did peers living with married parents. Children living with single and divorced parents also scored higher in problem behavior than did peers from intact families. An AAP task force concludes that children living with cohabiting parents are generally worse off than are peers reared by married parents. "Cohabitation," remark the AAP physicians, "is more unstable for children than either married 2-parent or single-mother families and tends to produce worse outcomes for children." One of the worst outcomes is that of abuse, which the AAP scholars note has been linked to living "with a mother and a cohabiting boyfriend."[41]

Scrutiny of data collected in 1999 from a nationally representative sample of 35,938 children (ages six to eleven) and adolescents (ages twelve to seventeen) reveals that "those living outside of two-biological-parent married families tend to report more behavioral and emotional problems and less school engagement." The data provide little to reassure those who suppose cohabitation serves society just as well as wedlock: in households headed by cohabiting couples (whether never-married cohabitors or step-parent cohabitors), children suffer from psychological, behavioral, and academic problems at significantly higher rates than are seen among peers living with two biological married parents. Though the distinctively high incidence of problems among young children in homes headed by cohabiting parents can be statistically attributed to economic circumstances, economic variables do not account for the high incidence of problems among adolescents in households headed by cohabitors. In any case, economists find that cohabiting parents spend less of their income on their children's education and more on their own tobacco and alcohol habits than do married peers. The researchers interpret this pattern as troubling evidence that cohabiting parents are less willing to invest in their children's future than are married parents.[42]

. . . or communal households—
children do predictably worse.

Communal childrearing also falls short. In ways predicted by attachment theory, children reared in the communal arrangements of Israeli kibbutzim experienced deleterious delays in their emotional and intellectual development. Psychological analysis of these delays focuses particularly on the psychological effects of communal sleeping, which kibbutzim leaders arranged as part of a communal upbringing that entailed "the collective's taking away from [parents] the lion's share of authority and responsibility for their children's care." The researchers judge the kibbutzim's communal-sleeping practice as "a social experiment in nature that was predestined to fail . . . because it employed sociocultural imperatives running counter to basic human needs."[43]

Other psychological data reveal further harmful effects of the out-of-home sleeping arrangements that were part of communal childrearing in Israeli kibbutzim. This communal childrearing arrangement resulted in "adverse effects on the quality of infant-mother relationships." As a consequence, adolescents reared in this way were "more vulnerable to becoming disorganized/disoriented." The researchers characterize the communal childrearing practice as one that "significantly deviates from the environment of evolutionary adaptedness." To assess the effects of various types of childrearing, researchers compared adolescents reared in communal kibbutzim settings with peers reared in familial kibbutzim settings, with peers reared in cities, and with peers raised in a communal setting as young children but moved to familial arrangements before age six. Those adolescents reared entirely in a communal kibbutzim setting manifest "less competent coping" when faced with separations than did the other three groups of adolescents.[44]

6

Gifts of the Natural Family

MARRIAGE AND MARITAL PARENTING provide incomparable gifts to all human societies. Again, we turn to statements found in the manifesto and to the scientific evidence supporting these ideals and truths.

Married, natural-parent homes bring health, . . .

"Marriage," an American Academy of Pediatrics task force explains, "is beneficial in many ways," in large part because "people behave differently when they are married. They have healthier lifestyles, eat better, and monitor each other's health." National health data also indicate that children of married parents enjoy significantly better health than do children of divorced parents. The same data set shows that "marital status is related to the health status of all the family members, including both parents and children." Writing from another perspective, a University of Maryland medical researcher blames parental divorce for causing or exacerbating various chronic diseases—including cardiac disease—among children. In addition, economic and medical data indicate that the upsurge in the number of single-parent, female-headed households has pushed an alarming number of children into both poverty and ill health. The poverty that is associated with "the loss of the wage-earning power of the absent parent, usually the father," predicts "higher rates of poor health and chronic health conditions in children," resulting in higher hospitalization and mortality rates among affected children. Finally, a team of Harvard epidemiologists identifies the distinctively high incidence of both physical and mental illness among the children of divorced and never-married parents as the reason that these children require pediatric and psychiatric services significantly more often than do children of married parents.[1]

. . . learning, . . .

The intact home is best predictor of true learning. In academic data collected from 349 young adolescents, researchers found that family structure is superior to any competing theoretical perspective in explaining children's academic achievement. Children in intact families consistently earn higher grades and engage in problem behavior less often than peers in single-parent or step-families. An Ohio State sociologist adduces evidence that "family structural effects" account for much of the "quite substantial" gaps in academic performance separating minority students from white peers. Because "living with both natural parents is positively associated with academic performance" for all ethnic groups and because fewer minority children than white children live with both natural parents, almost one-third of the black-white differential in math achievement and two-fifths of the black-white differential in reading achievement can be traced to differences in family structure. Allowance for the same factor actually shrinks the Hispanic-white gap in reading achievement to statistical insignificance. In data collected for the 1994 through 1999 versions of the British Household Panel Study, a strong linkage emerged between educational achievement and family structure. Compared to peers from other types of households, adolescents who grew up in households with both biological parents were more than twice as likely at age sixteen to achieve five passing marks on the General Certificate of Secondary Education and at age nineteen to achieve two A-level passes for their academic performance.[2]

. . . and success to the offspring reared therein.

The future of young people is mediated through their homes. In sophisticated multivariable statistical models, intact-family structure consistently predicts positive changes for students as gauged by researchers' composite Success Index. Other scholars conclude that young men and women from single-parent and step-parent families significantly fall short of the educational attainments and occupational status typical of peers reared in intact families. Not surprisingly, then, national income data indicate that young men and women reared by both biological parents earn significantly more in adulthood than do peers from other family backgrounds. Occupational attainment consistently runs significantly higher for the offspring of intact families than for peers reared in other household arrangements.[3]

Science shows that these same homes give life, . . .

Looking at data for a group of industrialized nations in Western Europe, North America, and Eastern Asia, Princeton University scholars found that married men and women lived longer on average than unmarried peers (never-married, divorced, and widowed) in all of them. Though the mortality advantage was greater for married men than for married women, it was significant for both sexes and actually increased in recent decades. Two national health surveys conducted in France provide data indicating that married mothers with children at home enjoy the kind of health improvement predicted by "role enhancement" theory. In contrast, single mothers suffer from "very unfavorable outcomes in terms of perceived health and malaise symptoms." In medical data collected from 7,524 white women age sixty-five or older, epidemiologists uncover strong evidence that marriage lengthens women's lives. Indeed, the researchers identify marital status as "the most consistent predictor" of mortality rates for the women involved in this study. Meanwhile, data collected as part of the National Longitudinal Mortality Study establish that when compared to divorced and single men and women in every age group, married men and women enjoy a statistically significant mortality advantage. Differences in economic background only partly account for this mortality advantage. And scholars at The RAND Corporation and the University of California-Riverside have established a clear statistical linkage between "experiencing parental divorce in childhood and a subsequently increased mortality risk."[4]

. . . wealth, . . .

Families create and share wealth. Drawing on nationally representative data collected between 1968 and 1992, Cornell and University of Washington scholars find a very strong linkage between marital status and income, showing a "substantial marital effect on the likelihood of experiencing one or more years of affluence during the life course." The researchers suggest that the wealth-fostering effect of wedlock crosses racial and gender lines, showing up for both whites and blacks, both men and women. Indeed, in statistical terms "the power of marriage to deliver affluence for women is extremely strong." The researchers see marriage fostering affluence by eliminating some of the household expenses that two single individuals would incur and by making possible "a division of labor that maximizes family income" by "enabl[ing] the partner with higher earnings [usually the husband] to devote relatively more energy and attention to remunerated work." Using nationally representative retirement data from 1992, Purdue economists also demonstrate that "being married has a large effect on household wealth," with unmarried individuals experiencing a 63 percent reduction in total wealth over the life course when compared with married peers. Separated, never-married, divorced, cohabiting, and widowed men and women all have "significantly lower wealth than the currently married," the differential being most pronounced for the separated and never married and least pronounced for the widowed. The investigators reason that marriage fosters the accumulation of wealth because "it provides institutionalized protection, which generates economies of scale, task specialization, and access to work-related fringe benefits, that lead to rewards like broader social networks and higher savings rates."[5]

Indeed, the wealth-creating benefits of marriage mark the best way out of poverty. Parsing data collected in 1995 from a national probability sample of 10,847 women ages fifteen to forty-four, researchers from Ohio State and Penn State Universities adduce evidence that "marriage matters economically": compared to never-married peers, "ever-married women are substantially less likely to be poor, regardless of race, family disadvantage, nonmarital birth status, or high school dropout." Moreover, the data collected by the authors of the new study indicate that "the deleterious effect associated with a disadvantaged family background is completely offset by marrying and staying married (i.e., disadvantaged and non-disadvantaged women who marry have similarly low odds of poverty)." This means that "marriage . . . offers a way out of poverty for disadvantaged women." The numbers bear this out. Married black women are much better off economically than are their single peers. The household net worth of the average married black woman in 1990 was $15,650, compared to just $4,563 for the average unmarried black woman.[6]

. . . and joy to wives and husbands, as well.

Building a marriage, rearing children, maintaining a home—all take effort and sacrifice. The marital bond can also bring disappointment and sorrow. All the same, true happiness and marriage go together. Psychological survey data collected from 3,032 randomly selected English-speaking American adults clearly indicate that the optimal state of mental health labeled "flourishing" is "more prevalent" among the married than among the unmarried (20 percent of the married, compared to 15 percent of the widowed, 13 percent of the never married, 12 percent of the separated, 10 percent of the divorced). In contrast, the mental state that the researcher calls "pure depression" shows up much less frequently among the married than among the unmarried (8 percent of the married, compared to 10 percent of the widowed, 11 percent of the never married, 13 percent of the divorced and 18 percent of the separated). Similarly, the percentage of individuals identified as both "languishing" and being in depression runs much lower among the married than among the unmarried. The researcher concludes that even after accounting for differences in socioeconomic background, married individuals are still more likely than the unmarried to enjoy "very good or excellent" mental and emotional health.[7]

Parsing national survey data, another researcher uncovers evidence that marital status has a strong influence on perception of well-being for both men and women, with "married people report[ing] they were more satisfied in life than unmarried people were, irrespective of gender." Although some theorists have asserted that wedlock benefits men more than it benefits women, this researcher finds that "married women [actually] scored higher than married men on perception of well-being." And in a survey of seventeen nations (including the United States, Japan, Spain, and Norway), married men and women report significantly higher levels of personal happiness than do their unmarried peers. The researchers interpret their findings as "perhaps the strongest evidence to date in support of the relationship between marital status and happiness." Contrary to feminist claims that wedlock benefits only men, the statistical results again show that "marriage protects females just as much from unhappiness as it protects males." And although the men and women in nonmarital cohabitation were happier in this international survey than were single men and women, their happiness still came in at "less than one quarter of [that] of married persons," further suggesting that "marriage protects more against unhappiness than does cohabitation."[8]

Disease, . . .

National health data indicate that divorced parents and their children suffer from significantly poorer health than do children of married parents. The same data set indeed shows that "marital status is related to the health status of all the family members, including both parents and children." National survey data collected between 1979 and 1995 in Great Britain and Sweden show that single mothers suffer from "significantly poorer health than couple mothers" in both countries, with the differential remaining "fairly constant" over the study period. Despite the particularly generous welfare benefits available to single mothers in Sweden, "the health disadvantage of Swedish lone mothers is substantial and is of similar magnitude to that of British lone mothers." Puzzled, the researchers speculate that Swedish single mothers might be suffering from poorer health than married mothers because of "lower access to social support."[9]

. . . depression, . . .

The absence of family bonds is a source of sorrow. Data collected for single and married mothers living in Ontario reveal a clear psychological disadvantage for unmarried mothers. Compared to their married peers, unmarried mothers are "almost three times more likely to have experienced a major depressive disorder." Compared to married mothers, single mothers are also more likely to have experienced an early onset of depression and to have had a recurrence. In a study initially focused on the mental-health effects of work environment, researchers discovered that for both men and women marital status actually predicts resistance to depression more reliably than does the quality of work environment. Among men, the likelihood of a major depressive episode ran an astounding nine times higher among the unmarried than among the married. A similar but less dramatic pattern was documented among the women in the study, unmarried women being particularly vulnerable to dysphoria (a form of depression), diagnosed three times as often among unmarried women as among their married peers. Unmarried men and women in fact suffer from more depression and anxiety than do married peers even when those married peers have experienced as many or more traumatic events in their lives. Furthermore, regardless of gender, unmarried adults feel less in control of their lives than do married peers. Data collected over a sixteen-year period for 1,380 adolescents and young adults show that compared to married peers, unmarried men and women suffer from significantly more depression and alcohol problems. "No social variable," the researchers conclude, "is more consistently related with the distribution of psychopathology than marital status."[10]

*. . . and early death come
to those who reject family life.*

Historical data from 1,961 male graduates of Amherst College born between 1832 and 1879 provides strong evidence that "marriage improved survival prospects [for these nineteenth-century men] even after controlling for health status in early adulthood." The self-selection evident in the failure of sickly men to marry did not come close to accounting for the mortality advantage enjoyed by the married: wedlock itself clearly lengthened life. Current data collected as part of the National Longitudinal Mortality Study establishes that when compared to married peers, divorced and single men and women in every age group suffer from a statistically significant mortality disadvantage. Differences in economic background only partly account for this mortality disadvantage.[11]

*Women are safest physically when
married and living with their husbands.*

Women who live with partners in non-marital arrangements expose themselves to real risk. Contrary to the predictions of feminist theory, domestic abuse (verbal, psychological, and physical) occurs significantly more often among lesbian couples than among heterosexual pairs. Surveys indicate that women who have been in both lesbian and heterosexual unions received significantly more abuse in the lesbian relationships. Nearly one-half of lesbians surveyed reported "being or having been the victim of relationship violence." Almost two-fifths of lesbians surveyed admitted having used violence against a partner. The researchers suggest that "the academic community . . . shares some of the blame for ignoring same-sex domestic violence," likely because of "a reluctance to challenge feminist frameworks." Researchers also find that males who cohabit express a distinctively "tolerant view of rape," evidently because they are "more accepting of violence and control" than non-cohabitors. Such attitudes suggest that "cohabiting women are at risk of physical violence" from their partners.[12]

Another researcher finds in national survey data a much higher incidence of domestic violence among cohabiting heterosexual couples than among married couples. Analysis indicates that cohabitors are more violent than married couples in large part because they are more socially isolated than are married peers. Although a pair of researchers began their work hypothesizing that domestic violence would occur less often among cohabiting couples than among the married, they have acknowledged that national survey data dramatically contradicts this hypothesis: compared to married peers, cohabiting women in this study are almost four times as likely to suffer "severe violence." A similar study finds cohabiting women to be almost five times as likely to experience "severe violence." This elevated level of violence among cohabiting couples cannot be accounted for as a consequence of household income, education, age, or occupation. Examining data from 724 randomly selected Buffalo-area women ages eighteen to thirty, researchers similarly find that, compared to married or single peers, cohabiting women are also more likely both to have used illicit drugs and to have experienced Intimate Partner Violence.[13]

> *Children are best sheltered from sexual,*
> *physical, and emotional abuse when they*
> *live with their married natural parents.*

The power of natural parents to protect their children can be stunning. Child abuse data from Canada show that preschool-age children living with a step-parent are forty times more likely to become child abuse victims than are those living with both natural parents. Indeed, sociobiologists identify stepchildren as distinctively vulnerable to abuse, giving substance to the wicked stepmother stories. The evidence indicates that when "given the choice between abusing a stepchild and a biological offspring, [abusers] never abused their own kin." American survey data reveal that single mothers are 71 percent more likely to visit "very severe violence" upon their children than are their married peers. Unmarried fathers are even more likely to act violently toward their children, particularly if they are impoverished. Overall, the researcher concludes that, compared to married peers, single parents are distinctly likely to harm their children "no matter what the economic situation."[14]

Natural family homes are also havens of protection against sexual abuse. Examining survey data collected in 1995, researchers discern an elevated rate of sexual abuse for children not in the care of both biological parents. Among children not living with both biological parents, 7.4 percent were reported to have experienced sexual abuse at some time in their lives, and 2.9 percent were reported to have experienced such abuse within the last year. Among children living with both biological parents, only 4.2 percent were reported to have experienced sexual abuse at some time in their lives, and only 0.9 percent were reported to have experienced such abuse within the last year.[15]

Consequently, American adults are especially likely to report having been sexually abused as children if they were reared in the absence of one of their natural parents. Men are particularly likely to have been sexually abused during boyhood if they were reared by a single mother. Women are distinctively more likely to have been sexually abused during childhood "under all family circumstances except that of living with two natural parents."[16]

Early abuse has long-term educational effects. Northwestern scholars conclude that young men and women from single-parent and step-parent families fall short of the educational attainments and occupational status typical of peers reared in intact families. Apparently, the violence often experienced by teens from broken homes forms the first link in "a chain of adversity" in which "victimization undermines academic performance, educational attainment, labor force participation, occupational status, and earnings in early adulthood."[17]

Fusionist conservatism has shown real
economic results in those family businesses
that successfully balance the pursuit
of profit and the integrity of homes.

Family businesses tend, as one might expect, to be family-friendly. Recent analysis shows how family businesses benefit society in ways that other businesses cannot. Because those who run family businesses seek more than merely financial profit, they can humanize a free-market economy. The large number of family enterprises in

Japan, for example, has helped to foster the benevolence and good-will that modify the effects of the profit motive. The consequence is that Japanese industry is much less of "a cut-throat jungle" than it would be in the absence of these family enterprises. In the family-owned Cadbury company, historians see a flat contradiction to Marxist theorizing about how capitalist employers invariably exploit employees. In this family business, a spirit of "benevolence without autocracy prevailed" in ways that "tempered capitalism" by maintaining good-will and solidarity in an environment in which "workers had the first claim on their employers' benevolence." Business analysts also fail to find evidence of the oft-assumed profit-kinship conflicts inherent in family business. Rather, their investigation reveals that family members working for small family businesses are satisfied with their careers and remarkably committed to their employment. Quite simply, working in a family business offers "more advantages than disadvantages."[18]

Unless guided by other ideals, corporations seek cheap labor wherever it can be found and an end to all home production. The whetting of appetites commonly takes precedence over family integrity in corporate advertising.

Globalization can be a danger to a family-centered social order. Anthropologists interpret the conversion of the entire world into "a global factory" as a new strategy developed by corporate leaders seeking cheap and relatively impotent labor. American industrial unions have lost much of their former strength because corporations have successfully converted capital mobility into a "new lever" of advantage. Cultural and economic analysis traces the "festering contradiction of modern womanhood" to the "displacement of crafts," which denied homemakers their traditional productive role by converting them into mere consumers in the capitalist market. Business analysts trace the displacement of community-based values to the triumph of exchange-based corporate values that intensify economic competition, so creating areas of high unemployment.

These exchange-based strategies are designed to satisfy shareholders, not to serve the community as a whole. As American and British corporations move many operations to Asia, Eastern Europe, and elsewhere, the middle class has contracted. Indeed, the median income in 1994 of an American family with two children was 33 percent lower (in inflation-adjusted dollars) than it was in 1973. As more and more U.S. corporations "go global," more American workers will lose their jobs even as more peasants in other countries lose their lands to technologically-driven agriculture. U.S. taxpayers continue to subsidize this process through corporate tax breaks. One analyst highlights the ways in which corporate giants are shedding millions of jobs in the United States and outsourcing production to countries such as Bangladesh or India. Corporations are thus shifting income from workers to investors, while shifting costs from investors to communities. Social disintegration—including family disintegration—is inevitable.[19]

We point to an inherent dilemma in capitalism:
the short-term interest of corporations in
weak homes and universal adult employment
versus the long-term interest of national
economies in improved human capital.

The flashpoint here is the employment of mothers. Data collected for middle-class grade school students show that "the more hours that mothers worked, the lower the children's grades and the poorer their work habits and efforts." What is more, "as mothers worked more hours . . . the children displayed less resilience, resourcefulness, and adaptability in the classroom." Another investigation found that "children of employed mothers, regardless of the mother's occupation, have somewhat lower probabilities of graduating from high school and college than do children of nonemployed mothers. The children of the average employed mother also have somewhat lower chances of going to college than do the children of nonemployed mothers." This pattern of educational disadvantage for the children of employed mothers holds for all but the children of very highly placed professional mothers.[20]

Academic data for 13,881 students show that children perform worse in mathematics if their mothers are employed full-time than if their mothers are employed only part-time or not at all. The researcher interprets this pattern as evidence that maternal employment adversely affects "the amount of social capital available to the child." Statistical analysis also demonstrates that a mother's market work has a "significant negative effect" on her children's school performance. The analyst regards this finding as evidence of a conflict between "a market career for women" on the one hand and "enhanced child development" on the other. Indeed, a demographer suggests that the rising level of employment for married women and the concomitant erosion of men's employment status means "the unraveling of America's social heritage."[21]

Movement of married women into wage competition with men also means the end of a family model premised on "specialization and exchange," a model in which women specialized on home production and their husbands concentrated on employment for wages. The new family model based on economic androgyny translates into low fertility and marital instability. Furthermore, economist Jennifer Roback Morse argues that a society full of *homines economici* cannot turn infants into the fully formed and moral adults necessary to sustain a healthy social order. Only the loving family sufficiently transcends economic imperatives to rear adults fit for ordered liberty.[22]

We marvel at fresh inventions that portend
novel bonds between home and work.

Computer-centered work at home portends a better future. White-collar workers who avail themselves of telecommuting technology in order to work at home generally feel they are better able to balance family and work responsibilities than do office-based peers. Many home-based telecommuters feel their arrangement reduces home-work conflicts and allows them to draw closer to their children or grandchildren by spending more time with them, particularly at critical junctures in the day (such as when children first return home from school). Survey and interview data collected from teleworkers employed in three Canadian organizations provide further evidence supporting a "positive" assessment of the impact of teleworking on family-work relationships. The teleworkers in the study report that starting teleworking significantly reduced the number of problems they experienced in managing family time. Finally, survey data from IBM telecommuters indicate that the majority of teleworkers judge their arrangement to be beneficial for family life. Many favor the arrangement because it allows them "to be with their children more frequently and in a wider range of activities."[23]

*We are inspired by a convergence of religious
truth and the evidence of science.*

A new president of the American Sociological Association hails the
emergence of fresh "theoretical intersections" connecting religion
and social science, identifying the study of family structures as one
of the places that these new intersections hold particular promise.
Important pioneering work in the new synthesis of social science
and religion can be seen in research by Catholic sociologists who
have devoted themselves to methodologies and perspectives that
harmonize with the tenets of their faith. Indeed, sociologists of
the family are increasingly turning to religion as an interpretive
grid for family research, opening "a bright future for religion and
family research." Though himself skeptical of religious metaphys-
ics, even sociobiologist E.O. Wilson sees religion serving a vital
biological function by reinforcing "allegiance to tribe and family."
Thus "God's will . . . coincides with Darwinian fitness."[24]

*Today's young people were born into
a culture of self-indulgence, of
abortion, a culture embracing death.*

Too many of the young have been indoctrinated in an anti-family worldview. Sociologist Daniel Spicer identifies in the linkage
of permissive attitudes toward pre-marital sex, non-traditional
gender roles, and abortion, "a web of linked and interdependent
deep-seated beliefs." These attitudes are not discrete and sepa-
rable but rather part of a distinct "worldview." In data collected
by an inter-university consortium, researchers identify a pattern

connecting feminist attitudes toward gender roles and family life with higher approval of abortion, less support for childbearing, and more approval of suicide.[25]

More than all generations before, today's
young people have known the divorce of parents.

Divorce hits children with particular force. Data collected between 1968 and 1997 shows that the probability of fathers' nonresidence with their children doubled during this period. Caused by rising rates of divorce and out-of-wedlock childbearing, most of the startling rise in the probability of paternal nonresidence occurred during the late 1970s and the 1980s, leveling off since then. Because of some lacunae in their data, the researchers admit that the risk of father-child separation may not have actually stabilized during the 1990s and may actually be higher than their results show. U.S. census data also reveal a dramatic rise in the percentage of children living in a one-parent or a non-parental household. In 1960, just 12 percent of all American children (7.8 million out of 63.7 million) lived in a one-parent or a non-parental home. In sharp contrast, in 2003, 30 percent of all American children (22.1 million out of 73.0 million) lived in a one-parent or a non-parental home.[26]

Today's young people have lived
too often without fathers.

Fatherlessness spreads like a plague. According to the America Academy of Pediatrics, "paternal absence" is predictive of "multiple and sometimes lifelong disadvantages" that go far beyond "health problems" to include "problems with school attendance, achievement and completion; emotional and behavioral problems; adolescent parenthood; substance abuse; and other risk behaviors." The predominance of female-headed households is also statistically "associated with a particular ecology in which children and adolescents do not thrive." This unhealthy social ecology fosters high rates of infant mortality and juvenile delinquency and low rates of academic achievement and high school completion.

Social historian David Courtwright identifies the disappearance of married fathers from the inner city as "the root cause" of the sharp rise in violent crime among young inner-city black males during the latter half of the twentieth century. Because of the "breakdown in the familial mechanisms for controlling young men," Courtwright sees in the modern inner city the very same social pathology which once made America's western mining camps and cowtowns "the most tumultuous region of the expanding nation." But whereas intact marriages and social fatherhood finally came to and pacified the western frontier, they seem to be disappearing from "the riptide of modern history."[27]

For example, the disappearance of fathers pushes more and more households into poverty. As welfare reform moved single parents into employment in a strong economy, the poverty rate in single-parent families fell from 51 to 44 percent, after factoring in the effects of the Earned Income Tax Credit, between 1995 and 2000. The poverty rate remained above 40 percent, however, because of "the biggest underlying source of poverty and insecurity for single-parent families: the family must generally rely on the earning of one person—typically a low-skilled woman—for support." What is more, concerns remain about "what full-time work may mean for children if mothers would prefer to be caring for their children." In the final analysis, "the best solution [to the problems of single-parent families] might be to find a way to reduce the incidence of single-parent families in the first place."[28]

Adolescent boys reared in the absence of fathers are especially likely to end up in custody. In data collected between 1979 and 1994 for 2,846 young men, researchers limn a strong link between youth incarceration risk and father-absence. Even in statistical analyses that take into account household income and residential permanence, sons reared in mother-only families are nearly two times as likely to be incarcerated as peers from mother-father families. The risk that adolescent boys and girls will engage in early sexual experimentation is also affected by family structure on two levels. First, adolescents (male and female) are especially likely to engage in early sex if they are themselves being reared in a single-parent or step-parent home. Second, the likelihood that adolescents will engage in early sex increases as the percentage of single-mother homes in the area rises. The researchers theorize that "the prevalence of single-mother families among friends and classmates and the lack of responsible and successful male role models may socialize youth to view early sexual behavior as expected and of little consequence."[29]

The sense of alarm grows. A pediatrician reports that inner-city children living in households headed by single mothers suffer with intolerable frequency from diseases (such as bacterial meningitis, rheumatic fever, and iron-deficiency anemia), neglect, abuse, crime, and homelessness. Economists at the Institute for Research on Poverty also identify the sharp increase in the number of single-parent families since 1970 ("the great majority" being mother-only families) as a prime reason that "the economic position of the working poor has stagnated or declined" in recent decades.[30]

Today's young people are the victims of a kind
of cultural rape: seduced into early sexual
acts, then pushed into sterility.

Two sociologists of the family lament the cultural triumph of the "greedy organism of the self," a triumph fostered by a "therapeutic individualism" legitimizing personal self-indulgence. Inevitably, such a cultural dynamic entails a "devaluation of children" because of the "restriction on one's freedom" that comes with childrearing. This unhealthy cultural dynamic encourages young adults to keep "control over [their] life and [their] time" by remaining childless.

Demographers investigating the "fertility crisis" in the industrialized world see anti-natal pressures in a global economy, which surround potential parents with "the almost limitless temptations of the modern consumerist society" but which endow children with "no immediate economic value [for] their parents." These investigators also emphasize the effects of "post-modern values" that foster non-marital sexuality but not marital childbearing. And these values have consequences. In interviews conducted in 1993, the majority of two hundred women in New England colleges expressed a desire to marry and have a family. In follow-up interviews seven years later, the majority of these women (now approaching thirty) were still single and childless.[31]

7

Introspection and Confession

Two decades after conservative Christians charged into the political arena, bringing new voters and millions of dollars with them in the hopes of transforming the culture through political power, it must now be acknowledged that we have failed. We failed not because we were wrong about our critique of culture, or because we lacked conviction, or because there were not enough of us, or because too many were lethargic and uncommitted. We failed because we were unable to redirect a nation from the top down. Real change must come from the bottom up or, better yet, from the inside out.

Cal Thomas, *Blinded By Might:Can the Religious Right Save America?*, April 1999.

I believe that we probably have lost the culture war. . . . in terms of society in general, we have lost. This is why, even when we win in politics, our victories fail to translate into the kind of policies we believe are important. . . . I know that what we have been doing for thirty years hasn't worked, that while we have been fighting and winning in politics, our culture has decayed into something approaching barbarism. We need to take another tack, find a different strategy.

Paul Weyrich, open letter to the social conservative movement, February 16, 1999.

We have failed. Our side, the "pro-family," "conservative," "traditional" side, has failed in our collective attempt to hold at bay the advancement of organized homosexuality. The "gay rights" movement has proceeded relatively unabated . . . and in precisely the arenas where we, the self-proclaimed political leaders of traditional Americans, have made it a point to engage the problem. We have failed *not* because we are any less intelligent, any less sophisticated, or any less committed than our opponents. . . . It is time we look in the mirror and ask ourselves some tough questions, not the least of which is, what is the world getting for all our investment?

Paul T. Mero, "Where We Stand," *Center Point* paper, The Howard Center for Family, Religion, and Society, June 1998.

THESE JUDGMENTS all came in the late 1990s, during the dot-com investment frenzy, the sex scandals and impeachment of President Clinton, and the unraveling of the Newt Gingrich "revolution" in the U.S. Congress. Do these judgments still hold?

One could possibly paint a brighter picture today. In retrospect, 1996 had brought two important changes in public policy that have had significant effects on the family. Tax reform that year implemented the new child tax credit, then $400 per child; today, it's $1,000 per child. This proved to be a significant step toward protecting family income and autonomy. Congress also embraced welfare reforms which reduced the incentives to out-of-wedlock births that were driving the growth of a fatherless underclass.

The optimist could list other recent positive developments. The "covenant marriage" idea has been implemented in several states, and may mark the beginning of the end of "no-fault" divorce. Steps have been taken to reduce the "marriage penalty" in federal tax law. The administration of George W. Bush has put persons with solid pro-family credentials in key posts at the Department of Health and Human Services and the State Department. U.S. ambassadors to key United Nations committees have largely brought a halt to anti-family initiatives there. Federal judges with apparent pro-family sentiments have won confirmation to key courts, notably John Roberts and Samuel Alito on the U.S. Supreme Court. We celebrate these gains.

All the same, we sense that darker currents are still at work in our time, and that recent victories have done little to counter the deeper sweep of change. In the United States, the marriage rate continues to fall. The proportion of new babies born out of wedlock rises again. Pornography, once confined to urban back allies, now pours into homes through the internet, creating a terrible new kind of addiction. "Family homes," defined by the presence of both a married couple and children, now comprise less than 25 percent of all American households.

Most dramatically, the "gay rights" campaign moves from legal victory to victory. Pro-family successes in state referenda that define marriage as only between a man and a woman obscure the more important change. Homosexuality has won cultural and legal acceptance as a legitimate lifestyle. Homosexuals can adopt children in most states. Schools commonly teach the gay agenda. Sodomy enjoys constitutional protection. Even the proposed Federal Marriage Amendment would allow states to craft registered partnerships for homosexual couples. In Europe, "gay marriage" spreads even into historically Catholic lands such as Spain.

In brief, Western culture still appears to be in decline, affecting the United States and many other nations. Secularization, the sexual revolution, the impact of industrialization, and the pressure of anti-family ideologies have all contributed to this decline. The iconic figures are there: from Charles Darwin and Karl Marx to Havelock Ellis and Sigmund Freud to Margaret Sanger and Margaret Mead to Alfred Kinsey and Hugh Hefner to Alva Myrdal and Paul Ehrlich. The "culture war" is not new. We are simply in a new phase.

Is such decline irreversible? As with radioactive substances, do all cultures possess a half-life? If so, then there would be no such thing as "failure" among those defending traditional culture. They would simply be playing out their pre-determined part. Yet if decline is not inevitable, then success would be defined by more than good deeds or good intentions.

For about thirty years, the contemporary "pro-family" movement has confronted an unrelenting onslaught of immorality, even depravity. The movement has fought tirelessly and valiantly. It has some victories to show for its efforts. And yet, in the larger context, it is losing—*we* are losing.

The Natural Family: A Manifesto rejects the idea of cultural, as much as economic, determinism. It rests on the premise that truths about morality, life, and purpose are unchanging. It holds that men and women—in any time or age—enjoy personal agency. They can make choices. They can strive to be better persons and to build a better culture. Renewal—personal and familial as well as cultural—is possible.

With this said, we believe it important to note certain mistakes within the movement—our movement—that have limited its effectiveness. Believing in the need for introspection, we ourselves confess to these weaknesses; we name no others.

*Too often, individual ambitions and squabbles
have prevented movement success.*

Authentic cultural renewal begins within individual families and in small communities. It cannot be accomplished through centralized institutions. For example, the educational renewal movement known as homeschooling began in hundreds of American kitchens, not in some grand building in the nation's capital. Showing a vital and pleasant anarchy, this movement has resisted all attempts at centralization, except for mechanisms of common legal defense.

To be effective, the "pro-family" movement needs to be decentralized as well. A presence in national capitols may be the last thing that we need. We should empower individual families to be informed and involved and then let them do their work.

Another error has been to strap our cause on the backs of personalities. A new form of worship spreads and people in the grassroots begin to look up to egos rather than in the mirror. An array of personal fiefdoms becomes the standing temptation. No one person makes or breaks any healthy movement. A victorious coalition is broad-based and equitable in its responsibilities and expectations. Our most successful efforts, such as stopping passage of the Equal Rights Amendment, occurred out in the states and involved legions of able volunteers. Phyllis Schlafly was the historical hero here. And she always acknowledged the more vital role of her grassroots colleagues and friends.

The essential problem is similar to the one faced by America's founding fathers. The "central government" must be capable, but limited. So should the organization of the pro-family movement. National bodies should provide a cohesive worldview and opportunities for learning, networking, and service. Nevertheless, the real work ought to be done in homes, neighborhoods, and small communities. To adapt a phrase, let a thousand initiatives blossom.

A narrowness of vision has led, at times, to a focus on petty questions, while the truly important battles have been ignored, and so lost by default.

Too many times, we have actually become the caricature of ourselves that is painted by our foes: partisan, uncaring, authoritarian, and greedy. In playing the game of politics, we have squandered credibility and respect. We have sometimes allowed the wholly unreasonable to occur in order to appear more compassionate and humane. In defense of "traditional culture," we have too often sounded arrogant, cold, and old-fashioned.

Part of the problem arises from the projection of private lives into public policy. Most people cannot separate the two. Unfortunately, public policy becomes distorted when citizens make their own lives a justification for dubious laws. Thus, someone who has gone through a rough divorce is likely to support divorce reforms designed to make divorce easy. Or a parent with a homosexual child might afterwards support public policies that legitimize or justify homosexuality. We make the same mistake when we project without caution our private religious beliefs onto public life, or when our own rhetoric adopts the language of moral crusade, or where we project our private lives as a public model.

We care that a man and a woman marry and bear children not because we want to impose our opinions on others but because this fosters social health. We are not telling people how to live; we are recognizing public policies that foster happiness, social peace, and prosperity. We are not imposing our preferences on others; we are trying to shape law and policy around normative arrangements justified by time and reinforced by biological and social sciences.

This is not to diminish the need for moral teaching or religious influence in society. To build an argument in terms of public policy or science is actually to enhance moral and religious argumentation. Not all persons think in a religious framework. We must use a language that the non-religious can understand. The burden is on us to help our neighbors understand the truth about the world's natural order, in ways that do not threaten them. Indeed, they should be inspired by our language.

We must also show them the distinction between the ideal and the real. We might, for instance, use a driving analogy. If you want to drive a car, you must follow the rules of the road. We are taught that the safest way to drive is to keep both hands on the steering wheel at all times, remain constantly alert to our circumstances, drive defensively, and obey all traffic laws. In truth, though, few of us live up to these expectations. We may drive with one hand on the steering wheel, talk on a cell phone, or drink a soda. We may exceed the speed limit. Add children in the backseat to the mix, and our falling short of the ideal is magnified once again.

So why do we hold on to such unrealistic expectations? Surely it would be easier to adjust the rules of the road to the actual driving experience? Yet we do not, for the predictable result would be more accidents, more deaths, more misery. Good public policy reflects ideal—not real world—driving behavior.

The same is true for public policy affecting marriage and family. We raise up the ideal of the natural family as dictated by human experience, knowing full well that no one will ever consistently achieve that ideal. When we ourselves fall short, when troubles afflict our family lives, it is not because we are hypocrites. It is because we are human.

This also frames the limits of public policy. The detailed regulation of someone's private life is not a matter of public policy, even when we foresee the trainwreck ahead. We might—and perhaps ought to—try to intervene privately. However, to maintain the delicate balance between personal liberty and community interests, we urge caution in applying the coercive powers of the state in private life.

We in the pro-family movement must understand this caution, even if our opponents do not. As matters of public policy, we care that men and women marry, bear children, and avoid divorce. But we should not care—in terms of public policy—why they marry, or whether they have a proper education about marriage, or (with a few obvious exceptions) how they rear their children, or how they manage their day-to-day conflicts. These are private matters, best left to the freedom we afford families to direct their own destinies.

We must also constantly remember that laws cannot turn around a nation. A good law is a reflection of a healthy culture. While the Supreme Court's decision in *Roe v. Wade* saddled the nation with abortion-on-demand, the truth is that wide sectors of the population welcomed the ruling. Even some prominent Christian conservatives of the era praised the *Roe* decision as a victory for religious liberty. Only Roman Catholic bishops vigorously dissented at the time.

Fighting now for new pro-life and pro-family Supreme Court justices is important, not least in the hope that *Roe* might be overturned. Still, all the pro-life justices in the nation will not overturn that decision if the nation's prevailing morality holds that abortion on demand is justified. The failed, if well-intentioned, efforts to prohibit the production and sale of alcohol in the United States pose a solid, even sobering example here. Our first priorities need to be reinforcing the structures of civil society and renewing a culture of marriage and family.

Strategic thinking and bold moves that could
transform key debates have been undone by timidity
on the part of leaders and funders.

We tell a true story here, withholding names. In 1997, two well-respected foundations, founded by well-meaning Christians, gathered dozens of America's pro-family leaders for a private summit to create a unified strategy to combat the encroaching anti-family culture. Many meetings convened over two years. The original gathering of fifty persons was whittled down to an executive committee of eight. Its task was to draft a strategic plan which would then be presented to the larger group and the foundations for approval and action.

Alas, the strategic plan never saw the light of day, let alone implementation. In place of a coherent strategy there emerged a ramshackle arrangement of individual projects. Indeed, the only unified aspect of the effort was a shared glee over the hope and promise of money for the individual projects.

Along the way, the committee *did* consider three revealing suggestions. The first was that the pro-family movement focus on what it stands for, not what it opposes. Over the previous three decades, we had shown what we were against: homosexuality, feminism, pornography, sex education, and so on. We had opposed virtually every cultural shift and modernist innovation. What we had not done very well was to say what we stood for, and why.

This idea was shot down in committee. The sobering fact which several persons alluded to was that pro-family groups raise money because of what they oppose, not because of what they support. The proposed focus on affirming a pro-family culture cut into an array of organizations whose financial health required slaying dragons daily. There is money to be made in dispatching terrible beasts; but little money for affirming a culture in which the dragons could not or would not exist. The situation also demands an unrelenting search for new dragons.

The second suggestion was that the strategic plan adopt the positive theme of the family as the fundamental social unit. This proposal, too, fell like a lead balloon. Astonishingly, the primary objection to it was that the family was not, in reality, the fundamental unit of society. This role, as one committee member felt, and several others didn't disagree, rightly belongs to the individual. (Indeed, this episode suggests a significant philosophical incoherence within the movement.)

The third suggestion was to focus the strategy on influencing parents. Several committee members argued that parents were the real problem. Children, they said, were more conservative than their parents these days. The latter should be avoided. Efforts at change should focus on children, especially where they congregate most often, in the public schools.

To the credit of those behind the conclave, they knew instinctively that the old strategies had not worked and that they were hearing little that was new. To push the process along, the benefactors brought in an outside consulting firm to critique the movement. The firm's report was thorough. It held that (1) we have failed; (2) we have failed for specific reasons; (3) we must change our approach; and (4) many of the participating groups were incapable of changing their approach, and so became part of the problem.

The outside report was largely ignored. The ramshackle plan reappeared. The very patient and trusting benefactors placed seed money in the kitty. Efforts began to find broader financial support for the plan. None appeared. In less than six months, the seed money was gone. Everyone went their separate ways. A golden opportunity was lost.

We believe that any successful collaboration and cultural change will begin with a focus on what we are for, not what we oppose. It will affirm the natural family as the fundamental social unit as its guiding principle. And it will respect the primary role of parents in setting and maintaining healthy family structure.

Sustaining large institutions, rather than encouraging swift and effective agents, has been too common.

Having become acclimated to Washington, D.C., our movement has willy-nilly joined into the culture of contention, of partisanship. The preference is to fight, rather than to win. There must be an enemy, so that we are always right and they are always wrong; so that we are good and they are evil. And since evil cannot be persuaded, the contest can never end.

These pressures grew apparent in the work of the National Commission on Children, active between 1988 and 1991. Created by an act of Congress, the original outlook for a pro-family result from its work was dim. Of thirty-six members, a third would be appointed by the president of the United States, a third by the speaker of the House, and a third by the president pro-tem of the Senate. The latter two posts were held by Democrats, and they filled their twenty-four slots with modern liberalism's first team: the president of the National Education Association; the president of the American Federation of State, County, and Municipal Employees; the president of the Children's Defense Fund; the ambitious governor of Arkansas; and so on. The very liberal Jay Rockefeller, senator from West Virginia, became commission chairman.

The twelve Republican appointees of President Reagan's were generally less well known. And only seven or eight of them could be accurately labelled as in the pro-family camp. All the same, this small group did its homework. Its members attended the numerous hearings and working sessions. They befriended Senator Rockefeller and earned his trust. On several key issues, he even became a convert. When the left-leaning staff produced an early draft "final report" that subtly violated hard-won agreements, he rebuked the staff and told them to get it right. When the Democratic majority finally showed up en masse at the session where the Commission would vote on the final draft, they were appalled by the document they were presented. All the same, the senator took them into a closed room and twisted their collective arm.

The Democrats were appalled that a report they thought would focus on expanding government services for children instead focused on ways to strengthen families and empower parents. As Barbara Dafoe Whitehead of the Institute for American Values later explained: "The National Commission on Children's . . . major public policy proposal does not call for new or expanded services to children. The $1,000-per-child tax credit proposal both affirms parental responsibility and widens parental choice. By putting money into the hands of families themselves, the tax-credit empowers parents, not providers and bureaucrats." She continued: "The commission's 519-page final report is filled with the language of moral values. . . . this is not the official language of insider politics and legislative analysis. It is the everyday language of the kitchen table. . . . It is an important intellectual event that marks a major turn after decades of partisan wrangling over the relationship between cultural values and child well-being."[1]

Alas, as it turned out, others in the pro-family movement preferred a continuation of partisan wrangling. Intense pressure came from one large pro-family group to vote against the Report. Democrats could never do the right thing, it insisted. In order to keep up the intensity on which fund raising rested, there could be no victory. The quarrel was needed—not the win. Similar pressure for similar reasons also came from the White House of President George H.W. Bush. One pro-family commissioner who worked for this administration was told that he would be fired, "cut off" at his knees, and "never work in this town again" if he voted in favor of the Report.

While this story had a happy ending (despite the pressure, the Report won almost unanimous approval; the lone exception was the ambitious governor of Arkansas, who abstained), most others do not. Anyone who has been a lobbyist in Washington, D.C., soon learns the game. Your job security depends on keeping your clients in the hinterland in a constant state of fear: "Terrible things are about to happen here in Washington; only I can save you." The same is all too true for large organizations. Contention, not victory, is what the system thrives on.

Money, particularly "direct mail" money,
has become the measure of too many things.

The virtue of "direct mail" fundraising is that it can provide an organization with a reliable monthly revenue stream. And money, of course, is necessary for the functioning of any effective organization. All the same, it is the writing of direct mail copy that can turn otherwise genial people into the "bigots" that the other side so delights in mocking. Positive messages usually generate a poor return; fear sells.

It is also easy for money to trump mission. Pro-family groups are properly mission driven. But the very logic of direct mail requires that attention focus on the scariest issues, not the more important ones. Keeping the flow of money going can quickly become all-consuming. Mission disappears because it does not pay.

In the search for new funds, organizations sometimes draw in successful business leaders as trustees. Unfortunately, it sometimes happens that these business leaders intentionally put money before mission. That is what they do in their for-profit realm, a priority they fail to reverse in the non-profit domain. These well meaning business people might suppose that if a mission does not pay, then the mission is flawed. In consequence, we witness the push to place money ahead of mission. Ultimately, we see otherwise loyal adherents working unconsciously to undermine some very good organizations.

> *Doctrinal and sectarian differences on important,*
> *but tangential, questions have been allowed*
> *to obscure unity on the central issues of family*
> *and life. Our foes have celebrated as old fears*
> *and suspicions between religious groups have*
> *trumped potentially powerful new alliances.*

In some fundamental ways, America has been blessed by religious peace and cooperation. The religious clauses in the federal constitution ban religious tests for public office, protect the free exercise of religion, and prohibit the favoring of any one sect over others. The result has been an astonishing flowering of denominations and the continued strength of religious belief and behavior, long after secularism has come to dominate most other Western nations.

All the same, profound divisions continue to trouble efforts at inter-faith cooperation in defense of the family. Forty years ago, prominent Baptists and evangelicals applauded U.S. Supreme Court decisions overturning state laws that had prohibited the sale of contraceptives (*Griswold*) and abortion (*Roe*). They saw these laws as "Catholic" issues.

Today, conservative evangelicals and Baptists hold a much more positive view of Catholic natural law doctrine and have become aggressively pro-life on the abortion question (the contraception issues remain more problematic). Other forms of pro-family co-operation between Catholics and conservative Protestants have grown as well.

On occasions, the collaboration has spread further. During the 1990s, for example, American Catholics and evangelicals joined in a pro-family coalition at the United Nations that also included Latter-day Saints (Mormons) and even Muslims. They success-fully blocked UN efforts to make abortion and sodomy guaranteed human rights. The definition of the natural family adopted in Rome in May 1998, came from a group representing Catholics, Evangelicals, Lutherans, Mormons, Jews, Muslims, and even a Unitarian. The World Congress of Families II, held the following year in November, marked the high point of this cooperation.

Since the events of 9-11, though, this alliance has faltered. Old suspicions have returned. Theological questions that divide have taken precedence over the common interest in defending the natural family.

Our foes are never more cheerful than when old religious big-otries and fears rear up again, sowing discord in the pro-family ranks. Their opportunities for building a post-family order hostile to homes and children are never greater than when religious peoples let those things which divide them triumph over that which unites.

*The initiative on most questions
has been left to the other side.*

The pro-family cause also falls prey to an obligatory optimism. The unspoken rule is that we shall never admit failure. We can go down in flaming defeat on an issue, and this obligatory optimism prevents any learning from our mistakes or humble admissions that our approach might have been wrong. Our tendency is to sit back, smile, and say: "What do you expect? We were up against the liberal media as well as [pick your enemy]."

This has led to a false impression of effectiveness. As a consequence of our failure in political efforts, we constantly redefine success. For example, consider where we are on the issue of gay rights. Twenty years ago, the U.S. Supreme Court gave us the *Hardwick* decision upholding state anti-sodomy laws—a huge political victory. A year later, in 1987, we won again with a Congressional prohibition on the use of tax dollars to promote homosexuality.

In 1988, however, the omnibus "Ryan White" bill became law, undoing our victory the prior year. Federal funds to support the gay agenda began flowing. The Hate Crimes bill came next. For the first time, federal law equated "sexual orientation" with traditional suspect classes of people, along the lines of the Civil Rights Act of 1964. Also for the first time, President George H. W. Bush invited homosexual activists to the White House for the signing of the bill. Starting in 1993, the Clinton Administration partly opened the U.S. military to homosexuals ("Don't Ask, Don't Tell"); through regulatory acts, it completely opened the civil service ranks. In 1994, Congress again approved federal funds to support the gay agenda on a 234 to 194 vote (seven years earlier, *only forty-seven votes* were in favor, compared to 368 opposed). Our last redoubt, or line of defense, is now marriage; the chosen vehicle a constitutional amendment to restrict marriage to a man and a woman. Even here, though, we have yet to win even a simple majority in the Senate, let alone the sixty-seven votes needed.

Meanwhile, the U.S. Supreme Court affirmed the enigma of "sexual orientation" in its *Romer* decision, striking down a Colorado measure that had denied special status to homosexuals. A defense of the natural family now leaned toward "animus." Compounding this extraordinary shift was the Court's *Lawrence* decision in 2002, where it held that objections to homosexuality are "irrational." Through the same logic, sodomy became a protected constitutional right.

Many hope that the new "Roberts Court" will make a difference. Perhaps so. We fear, though, that it will at best slow the pace of change and not reverse the broad rights and privileges bestowed on "the gay community" and their diverse sexual allies over the last two decades.

The truth hurts. If we were a business, we would be bankrupt. If we were a sports team, we would be in last place. Obligatory optimism blinds us from confronting our string of losses, and looking for new approaches.

What might make a difference? One model of action that we raise up is the World Congress of Families. It recognizes that the battle in which we are engaged is universal in scale, but requires solutions only found in the hearts of persons of good will. It serves as a rallying center for the world's family systems grounded in religious faith. Confronting the militant secular individualism and the moral anarchy that has swept over the Western world, it fosters an international network of pro-family organizations, scholars, and cultural and political leaders who work to restore the natural family as the fundamental social unit. It affirms and builds a positive united front among the family-centered religious peoples, notably Christians, Jews, and Muslims.

The Congress also works to shift the terms of key public debates, with a focus on what we are for replacing a focus on what we oppose:

- We celebrate the creation of large families as special gifts (instead of "opposing abortion and population control").

- We raise up the Natural Family as the source of social renewal and progress (instead of "opposing new family forms").

- We proclaim religious orthodoxy to be the source of humane values and cultural progress (instead of "opposing secularism").

Another way of explaining the World Congress of Families (WCF) is to clarify both what it *is* and what it *is not*:

- The WCF *is not* a structure seeking to unify the world's pro-family and pro-life organizations under its guidance and control. It *is* a practical effort to build greater understanding and encourage informal networks among family advocates at the national and international levels.

- The WCF *is not* an "ecumenical" campaign seeking to advance its agenda by doctrinal compromise. It *is* a coalition of the most orthodox believers within each denomination, church, or faith group, persons who are the least likely to compromise on their core beliefs.

- The WCF *is not* an effort at crafting "one-world religion." It *is* a venue where religiously-grounded family systems can respond together in a positive manner to the global spread of a militant secularism that threatens the liberties and existence of all vital faiths.

- The WCF *is not* a massive organization with visions of power and permanence. It *is* a project currently coordinated by a small organization; it will continue only so long as it proves helpful to others and to the defense of the natural family.

The record of the first three congresses suggests that this model works. For example, the World Congress has already altered key terms of debate. The phrase, "traditional family," with its aura of "old-fashioned," is being replaced in national and world debates by "natural family," with its aura of energy. This has occurred globally.[2] Closer to home, American groups ranging from the Church of God to the American Legion have formally embraced the new terminology, and have used it as a basis for action.

Changing the terms of debate is the first step toward any moral, intellectual, and political victory. The World Congress of Families model has taken that step.

8

A Natural Family Policy

INSPIRED BY IDEALS, informed by science, our manifesto also lays out an agenda, a platform of action, a true family policy fit for the twenty-first century. While forward looking, our broad scheme draws inspiration from historical figures and proven political foundations.

We look to the example of Louis de Bonald, who stands for us as a hero. He confronted the social extremists of the French Revolution, denouncing proposed reforms that would weaken marriage and encourage divorce. As he explained in his 1801 book *On Divorce*, marriage was "natural" in a particular sense: "[I]t derives from the constitution of our being, of our nature, and is a natural act: for the true nature of man and the real constitution of his being consists in natural relationships with his being's author, and in natural relationships, both moral and physical, with his fellows."[1] He lost the argument in that year. In the wake of Napoleon's defeat, though, he led the successful effort to repeal the equivalent of "no-fault" divorce, restoring authority to the natural family.

We also look to the example of Edmund Burke. He, too, opposed the social radicalism of the French Revolution. He also affirmed the true foundations of ordered liberty, finding them in the web of association that gives purpose and direction to the individual. As he wrote in his 1791 *Reflections on the French Revolution*: "To be attached to the subdivision, to love the little platoon we belong to in society, is the first principle (the germ as it were) of public affections. It is the first link in the series by which we proceed toward a love to our country and to mankind. The interest of that portion of social arrangement is a trust in the hands of all those who compose it; and as none but bad men would justify it in abuse, none but traitors would barter it away for their own personal advantage."[2] These "little platoons" include villages, religious societies, colleges, and neighborhoods. However, it is the family resting on conjugal fidelity and fecundity that forms, energizes, and renews all the others.

We draw inspiration, as well, from the Dutch cleric and political leader of the late nineteenth century Abraham Kuyper. We share his analysis of the legacy of the French Revolution, an event which "proved to be not just a change in *regime* but a change of system, of political organization, of general human *theory*. In place of the worship of the most high God came, courtesy of Humanism, the worship of *man*. Human destiny was shifted from heaven to earth. . . . And *emancipation* became the watchword by which people tampered with the bond of marriage, with the respect children owe their parents, with the moral seriousness of our national manners."[3]

We also share Kuyper's concern over the imperialism of the industrial principle, which—if left to itself—seeks to intrude into all areas of life, including family relations: "So must everything become uniform, level, flat, homogenous, monotonous. No longer should each baby drink warm milk from the breast of its own mother; we should have some tepid mixture prepared for all babies collectively. No longer should each child have a place to play at home with its mother; all should go to a common nursery school."[4]

As did Kuyper, we call on nations to honor religion so as to protect "our standard of human life." We affirm freedom of conscience and religious liberty. We seek the restoration of "organic relations." This need not necessarily be with all the details found in, say, 1788 or 1957. However, it should be "on the basis of the family." And we urge that "the spirit of the Compassionate" fill public life, so that "our legislation may show a *heart* and officialdom some sympathy for suffering citizens; that powerless labor may be protected from coolly calculating corporate power; and that even the poorest citizen may count on the prospect of swift and sound justice."[5]

In addition, our policy prescriptions rest on the closely related principles of federalism and subsidiarity. Federalism dictates that political power should be divided between a central authority and smaller political units, such as provinces, states, cities, and townships. This division of powers marks each entity as both co-ordinate with and independent of the others, so that no one authority can claim the same level of power as found in a unitary state. Subsidiarity has received fullest expression in Catholic social teaching. As Pope John Paul II explained in the 1991 encyclical *Centesimus Annus*: "The 'principle of subsidiarity' must be respected. 'A community of a higher order should not interfere with the life of a community of a lower order, taking over its functions.' In case of need it should, rather, support the smaller community and help to coordinate its activity with activities in the rest of society for the sake of the common good." And at the base of this pyramid of small communities we find, once again, the natural family.

Our platform also builds on lessons learned from past episodes of family reconstruction. Notably, we admire the achievements of the American family model in the middle decades of the twentieth century. Between 1935 and 1965, the marriage rate climbed, the marital birthrate soared, the divorce rate fell after 1946, and measures of familial happiness rose. And yet, as noted in chapter 1, this renewal disintegrated over the next fifteen years.

Part of this failure can be attributed to the ideological assaults—feminist, Marxist, neo-Malthusian, "Playboy-ist"—that mobilized against the breadwinner/homemaker/child-rich family model. All the same, we see weaknesses that left the restored American family of the mid-twentieth century vulnerable.

- The new suburban family rested on an assumption of the "companionate" model of marriage, which emphasized psychological tasks such as "personality adjustment" and exaggerated gender roles (for example, the role of the "glamour girl" for wives[6]) to the exclusion of true complementarity and meaningful household functions.

- Homemaking women and adolescents were increasingly isolated in suburban developments without viable central places for the building of healthy community.

- Breadwinning men engaged in long commutes and were often only occasional figures in their homes.

- After 1945, policy-making elites failed to recognize America's mid-century family policy achievements, leaving them vulnerable. Specifically, when the "family wage" concept came under challenge, few were able or willing to defend it.

- African Americans never fully entered the family model of the 1950s, a failure ably dissected in Daniel P. Moynihan's famed 1965 report *The Negro American Family: The Case for National Action.*[7]

- Certain "internal contradictions" within the Social Security system also emerged, including disincentives to bear children and a hostility to direct intergenerational care.

- And the "family wage" scheme of the 1950s proved too rigid to accommodate complex human circumstances.

We need to do better.

Our platform also draws on recent examples of successful family policy. Starting in the *mid-1970s*, for instance, a growing number of American parents—for various reasons—turned to homeschooling. At first, they faced hostile state authorities: some were arrested, and some briefly imprisoned for seeking to reclaim this pre-modern family task. Yet the home education movement grew, and by the early 1990s had regained this natural right in all fifty states. By 2005, over two million American children were in home schools. The educational results have been impressive. More significant, though, are the social effects. Virtually all home-schooled students are in married-couple homes. And 77 percent of homeschooling mothers do not work for pay, compared to 30 percent of all mothers nationwide. Importantly, the fertility of these families is substantially higher than that of other families.

Sixty-two percent have three or more children, compared to only 20 percent nationwide. And slightly over a third (33.5 percent) have four or more children, compared to a mere 6 percent in all homes with children.[8] By rejecting "modern" state education, and by embracing "pre-modern" approaches, these American families have grown stronger and larger.

Second, about twenty years ago America also *re*discovered an alternative to state child allowances and paid parental leave, an approach that has a positive fertility effect. Specifically, after two decades of neglect, the U.S. Congress in 1986 nearly doubled the value of the personal income tax exemption for children to $2,000 per child, and indexed its value to inflation. Repeated studies have found that European child allowances—paid by the state to mothers as a monthly stipend for each of their children—have little positive effect on fertility. However, in the U.S., there is strong evidence of a "robust" positive relationship between the real, after-inflation value of the tax exemption for children and family size. Economist Leslie Whittington has actually calculated an astonishing elasticity of birth probability with respect to the income tax exemption of between .839 and 1.31. This means that a one percent increase in the exemption's real value results in about a one percent increase in birth probability in families.[9]

Why this difference? It appears that allowing families to keep more of what they earn while raising children—that is, turning children into little tax shelters—has a positive, even life-affirming psychological effect on parents that money coming from the state cannot replicate. In any case, a significant increase in overall American fertility coincides with the increase in the exemption's value in 1986. More recently, the rise in marital fertility, starting in 1996, correlates precisely with the introduction of a new, additional child tax credit that year. In other words, pro-family tax cuts appear to work.

Our platform builds as well on relatively favorable cultural conditions. Americans stand almost alone among modern nations as a people bound to active religious faith, and active faith commonly translates into larger families. The American system, which encourages the free exercise of religion while prohibiting the formal establishment of a state religion, has encouraged stronger religious sentiments.[10] At the most dramatic level, some religious communities still on the margins of American life—the German-speaking Old Order Amish found in rural communities in twenty states, the Hutterites in Montana and North Dakota, and Hassidic Jews in New York, Cleveland, and other cities—continue to report average completed family size in excess of six children. In addition, the fertility rate of the state of Utah is nearly twice the national average, reflecting an average of about four births per woman among Latter-day Saints or Mormons. Surveys also show that "fundamentalist Protestants" and traditional "Latin Mass" Catholics who attend religious services at least once a week also record higher total fertility.[11]

Finally, Americans are generally held less hostage to the anti-natal dogmas of pure "gender equality" than are the "Swedenized" Europeans. As the University of Virginia's Stephen Rhodes' book *Taking Sex Differences Seriously* reminds us, women and men are hardwired to be different. Denying these differences can only result in violations of human nature, doing particular harm to existing *and* potential children.[12] After decades of work by feminist ideologues to re-engineer human nature, some Americans remain resilient, open to the natural power of gender complementarity. For example, despite massive federal financial preferences and

incentives for putting small children in day care, over 60 percent
of new mothers avoid returning to full-time work and a third of
young mothers still find ways to remain home full-time with their
preschool children. And this proportion appears to be growing
again.[13] Phillip Longman even sees a "return of patriarchy," rooted
in the relative biological vigor of religious peoples.[14] The imperatives of biology, of human nature, are still active in the U.S.

A PRO-FAMILY FRAMEWORK

How might these lessons be applied in public policy?[15]

Marriage Policy

- Governments should re-introduce "fault" into laws governing divorce.

- States should treat marriage as a full economic partnership.
  In the United States, this would mean reintroducing full
  "income splitting" in the income tax, as existed between
  1948 and 1963. Such a measure would eliminate the most
  notorious "marriage penalty."

Population Policy

- All governments should recognize that strong families
  commonly rest on religiously-grounded morality systems,
  which deserve autonomy and respect as vital aspects of
  civil society.

- States should welcome large families, created responsibly through marriage, as special gifts to society, deserving
  affirmation and encouragement.

- All national governments and international entities should underscore that the demographic problem facing the twenty-first century is depopulation, not overpopulation.

Domestic Policy

- Income tax exemptions for children and child tax credits should be greatly expanded, indexed to inflation, and made universally available to families.

- Agencies promoting population control and diminution (such as Title x of the Public Health Services Act in the United States) should be shut down.

Infant and Toddler Care

- State subsidies and credits for daycare should also be available to parents who care for their preschoolers full-time, at home. A tax credit for this purpose should be refundable to those parents without the income to claim the full credit, allowing for a reduction in means-tested government daycare subsidies.

Education of the Young

- Home education should be protected. All relevant governments should reform their compulsory education laws along the model of the American state of Alaska, where any child is exempted who "is being educated in the child's home by a parent or legal guardian." This law precludes registration, reporting, or curricular requirements.

- Educational diversity should be encouraged in ways that reinforce family autonomy and school independence. "Tuition tax credits" are too narrow in their focus, giving no reception to home-educating families. "Vouchers" tend to make private and religious schools dependent on state funds, open these institutions to potential regulation, and subtly erode the virtues of personal and familial sacrifice, which are key to the success of independent schools.

- In place of vouchers, other measures deserve attention:

  - Per-capita child tax deductions and credits, without any link to schooling, should be preferred at all government levels; and

  - New tax credits on all forms of educational expense (including books, fees, tuition, and special lessons) should be created, with an Illinois law allowing a credit of 20 percent on such expenses up to five hundred dollars per year as a model; or

  - All educational expenses (from preschool fees and homeschooling expenses to university tuition) could be treated as an investment in human capital, logically enjoying full income tax deductability.

- To restore educational liberty and neighborhood integrity, all state school systems should be deconsolidated to single-school districts. These public schools, moreover, should be "open." Like an American community college, they should offer their learning and extra-curricula opportunities to all families in the district, but compel none. These schools would again be able to reflect the values of local communities and would have strong incentives to serve the neighborhood and its inhabitants.

Housing

- The need is to refunctionalize individual homes, abandoning governmental biases toward the frail "companionate model" of family home-design and opening urban, suburban, and rural life to a return of the "productive home." In the American setting, specific reforms would include:

  - Abolishing all mortgage underwriting rules that discourage the creation of home offices, home schools, and home businesses.

  - Ending those regulations of the professions—such as medicine, law, dentistry, and accounting—which favor giant institutions and prohibit decentralized learning through arrangements such as apprenticeships.

  - Loosening or abolishing zoning laws and restrictive covenants to allow the flourishing of home gardens, modest animal husbandry, home offices and businesses, and home schools.

Elder Care and the Bonds of the Generations

- True "intergenerational" reform would rebuild incentives that favor both childbearing and family-centered elder care, by restructuring incentives within the Medicare and Social Security systems. With America again as the example:

  - Taxpayers should be granted a credit of 20 percent against their total FICA (payroll) tax for each child born or adopted, a credit to be continued until the child reaches age thirteen. This would mean that a family with five children, ages twelve and under, would pay no FICA tax in that year (but would still receive all due employment credit).

- Taxpayers should be granted a 25 percent credit against their total FICA tax for each elderly parent or grandparent residing in the taxpayer's home.

- For each child born, a mother should receive three years (twelve quarters) of employment credits (calculated at the median full-time income) toward her future Social Security pension.

- A person should also receive one year's employment credit toward Social Security, at the same median income level, if he or she serves as the primary caregiver for an elderly relative residing in his or her home.

- Base FICA tax rates could be raised to accommodate these reforms at a revenue-neutral level (so shifting the tax burden onto those without children and/or refusing to care for their own); or the OASDI tax could be applied to all income and no longer capped off at incomes over $94,400 (as of 2006).

Child Welfare Policy

- All levels of government should protect parental rights in at least two ways: (1) laws and regulations should unequivocally endorse and reinforce the married, two-parent family as the fundamental unit of society, and (2) laws and regulations should unequivocally safeguard against the abuse of state power, particularly when it comes to terminating the constitutionally protected rights of parents.

- Of all the powers the state possesses in child welfare proceedings, the ability to terminate permanently the legal
rights of parents is the ultimate and most drastic. Allowing the state to do so on grounds less than parental fault
is inconsistent with the constitutional status of parental
rights.

- This would mean that the court must find by clear and
convincing evidence that the parent or parents have either
abandoned, abused, substantially neglected the child or
children, or are unfit or incompetent by reason of conduct
or condition which is seriously detrimental to the child
or children.

Divorce Policy

- Covenant marriage provides an attractive possibility for reform since it is voluntary for the parties involved. However,
this also may mean that it is more likely to attract couples
with a high level of commitment, whereas some couples
who most need legal incentives to make their marriage
work will not receive them. Other piecemeal reforms are
also attractive, especially those that recognize the severe
impact of divorce on children. These tend, however, to
focus on modifying the way a divorce takes place, not
discouraging a divorce in the first place.

- In the final analysis, only a forthright admission that no-
fault divorce is detrimental for couples, children, and society will be truly effective. The corollary of this admission
is that fault grounds need to be reintroduced into the law

of marital dissolution. This will allow the law to serve as a check on unilateral divorce and ensure that marriages are not dissolved for frivolous or trivial reasons. It will also signal to prospective married couples that the law expects them to take seriously their commitments and that they ought to think deeply and prepare well before marrying. As it shifts cultural trends, it can also provide assurance for children that their families will not be shattered unless they are really at risk. Given research that indicates that, over time, even couples in unhappy marriages will eventually begin to appreciate their partner again and experience a happy marriage, a change in the divorce culture might enhance the individual happiness of adults.

- The best public policy on divorce would reintroduce fault grounds where a marriage is longstanding or where children are involved. Accordingly, irreconcilable difference should not be grounds for divorce if: (1) there are living minor children of the marriage; or (2) the parties have been married ten years or longer; or (3) one of the spouses contests the divorce.

Family Impact Statements

- The increasing complexity and intrusiveness of the law and the increasing fragility of family relations argue strongly for a mechanism that maintains the core unit of society. A family impact statement is an important tool in maintaining this discipline, and is most likely to be successful if it: (1) recognizes the pre-existing nature of the family, (2) includes a normative definition of the natural family,

(3) includes a check on actions that would be unfriendly to the family, and (4) provides tools for assessing whether an action will maintain or undercut the family.

- A two-tiered approach with the enactment of family impact statement legislation and appointment of a commission to assess the impact of current law on the family could go far to ensure that a state is truly "family friendly."

Pornography

- States and provinces should allow divergent and diverse communities to regulate the existence, flow, and content of pornography and obscenity in their own way.

- The simplest way to do this is to increase the penalty for pandering obscenity from a misdemeanor to a felony. Most states only penalize pandering with a misdemeanor, hardly an incentive for prosecutors to spend precious time and resources on protecting communities from obscenity. Increasing pandering penalties from a misdemeanor to some degree of felony would create an incentive for prosecutors, already inclined to attend to these legal matters, to do so.

Taken together, we believe that this policy framework would undergird and encourage a stable, autonomous, child-rich, multi-generational, natual family system.

We can also point to very specific models of legislation that meet our criteria. For instance, the proposed "Parents' Tax Relief Act of 2006" (HR 3080, S 1305), introduced in the 109th U.S. Congress, would:

- Extend the existing child care tax credit to include stay-at-home parents with young children.

- Make the $1,000 child tax credit permanent, index it to inflation, remove income limits on eligibility, and extend the age of covered dependent children to eighteen.

- Eliminate the marriage penalty in the federal income tax, once and for all.

- Increase the personal income tax exemption for children to $5,000.

- Support home-based businesses and encourage telecommuting for parents.

- Extend Social Security work credits and benefits to stay-at-home parents.

We applaud this measure because it recognizes the value of the parental care of small children and expands the child care choices of all new mothers and fathers. It affirms marriage as a public good and restores recognition of the marital couple as an economic partnership. The bill properly affirms the value of children to the nation and responds to the extra economic burdens faced by young parents. This measure seeks to reduce conflicts between workplace and home by making it easier for the home itself to be a place for market labor. And the measure recognizes the full-time mother or father as individuals doing publicly valued work, deserving recognition within the Social Security system.

These approaches also avoid the mistakes of the European model. Most other developed nations provide state child allowances to parents as offsets to the costs of rearing children. As shown earlier, though, this method tends to make families wards of the state and to weaken marriage. In contrast, the "Parents' Tax Relief Act of 2006" uses carefully targeted tax policy measures to enable families to retain more of their *own* earned income while children are in the home. The record shows that this approach supports family formation and strengthens homes.

Viewed from another angle, this bill would also eliminate inequities that have crept into U.S. tax policy. For example, federal law currently gives a generous tax credit, or subsidy, without income limit to parents who purchase daycare. But existing policy gives no recognition at all to full-time parental child care which, social science shows, is predictably better for young children.[16] The "Parents' Tax Relief Act of 2006" would begin to set things right by granting a tax credit of $250 per month for families that make the financial sacrifice to have one parent serve as the full-time, at-home caregiver for children ages six and under. On the one hand, this measure creates a level playing field; on the other, it expands the child care choices of *all* qualifying families.

Second, the infamous "marriage penalty" remains alive and well. The tax cut of 2001 removed this penalty only for the 15 percent tax bracket. The "marriage penalty" still afflicts the majority of Americans in the middle and high tax brackets. The proposed bill would fully eliminate this penalty by making all tax brackets twice as wide for married couples as they are for singles.

Third, the per-child tax relief provided by the existing personal exemption and the child tax credit is inadequate, well below the relief delivered by the exemplary, pro-child Tax Reform of 1948. The proposed bill would raise the personal exemption for children to $5,000 and make permanent the $1,000 per child tax credit and index it to inflation, in order to protect its future value.

Reflecting old assumptions about the need for industrial centralization, federal tax policy still favors large central offices and factories over market labor in the home. This bill would simplify and expand the availability of the deduction for business use of the home and also encourage telecommuting. These are progressive ideas designed to increase family-friendly, home-centered work opportunities in the new information age.

Finally, the American Social Security system fails to recognize the full-time care of small children as real work (even the existing "homemakers" pension has no linkage to children). This is troubling, for there is strong evidence that existing incentives within Social Security discourage the birth of children,[17] even though such new children are in fact needed to maintain the system in the future. This measure boldly faces this problem by granting employment credit toward future Social Security benefits to those parents who make the sacrifices to raise their children, full-time, at home.

THE CALL

Authentic pro-family policy, though, only provides a legal and financial framework for social health and renewal. The flesh, blood, and spirit of a culture animated by the natural family ideal comes from those young persons ready to commit themselves to this vision of life. Accordingly, we conclude the manifesto with a special call to the young, "the ones with the power to make the world anew." They have lived through the disorders of the last several decades, and have witnessed the consequences in troubled or ruined lives. We point them to a different future: "You have the chance to shape a world that welcomes and celebrates children.

You have the ability to craft a true homecoming. Your generation holds the destiny of humankind in its hands. The hopes of all good and decent people lie with you." And we predict their success, for this fresh life is in harmony with human nature and the will of our Creator.

May it be so!

The Geneva Declaration (1999)

OUR PURPOSE

We assemble in this World Congress, from many national, ethnic, cultural, social and religious communities, to affirm that the natural human family is established by the Creator and essential to good society. We address ourselves to all people of good will who, with the majority of the world's people, value the natural family. Ideologies of statism, individualism and sexual revolution today challenge the family's very legitimacy as an institution. Associated with this challenge are the problems of divorce, devaluation of parenting, declining family time, morally relativistic public education, confusions over sexual identity, promiscuity, sexually transmitted diseases, abortion, poverty, human trafficking, violence against women, child abuse, isolation of the elderly, excessive taxation and below-replacement fertility. To defend the family and to guide public policy and cultural norms, this Declaration asserts principles that respect and uphold the vital roles that the family plays in society.

THE FAMILY AND SOCIETY

The natural family is the fundamental social unit, inscribed in human nature, and centered on the voluntary union of a man and a woman in the lifelong covenant of marriage. The natural family is defined by marriage, procreation and, in some cultures, adoption. Free, secure and stable families that welcome children are necessary for healthy society. The society that abandons the natural family as the norm is destined for chaos and suffering. The loving family reaches out in love and service to their communities and those in need. All social and cultural institutions should respect and uphold the rights and responsibilities of the family.

THE FAMILY AND MARRIAGE

The cornerstone of healthy family life, marriage brings security, contentment, meaning, joy and spiritual maturity to the man and woman who enter this lifelong covenant with unselfish commitment. In marriage, both husband and wife commit to a life of mutual love, respect, support and compassion. Spousal conflicts that can arise in marriage are opportunities for personal and marital growth, not, as modern cultures encourage, reasons to break the covenant. Divorce is destructive to families and society. Society and public policy should discourage divorce, while taking legal or other appropriate action in cases of intransigently abusive relationships. Steadfast commitment in marriage provides the security in family life that children need. Children also need and are entitled to the complementary parental love and attention of both father and mother, which marriage provides. Communities and religious institutions should care for families and households whose circumstances fall short of these ideals. Social policies should not promote single-parenting.

THE FAMILY AND CHILDREN

The natural family provides the optimal environment for the healthy development of children. Healthy family life fulfills the basic human need to belong and satisfies the longings of the human heart to give and receive love. The family informs the human person's original attitude toward such fundamental matters as identity, security, responsibility, love, morality and religion. In personal and intimate ways that no self-defining entity could, the natural family cares for its children and provides for their spiritual, physical, psychological and moral growth. Policy should promote the definition and permanence in family relationships that create the stability and security in family life children need.

THE FAMILY AND SEXUALITY

The complementary natures of men and women are physically and psychologically self-evident. These differences are created and natural, not primarily socially constructed. Sexuality is ordered for the procreation of children and the expression of love between husband and wife in the covenant of marriage. Marriage between a man and a woman forms the sole moral context for natural sexual union. Whether through pornography, promiscuity, incest or homosexuality, deviations from these created sexual norms cannot truly satisfy the human spirit. They lead to obsession, remorse, alienation, and disease. Child molesters harm children and no valid legal, psychological or moral justification can be offered for the odious crime of pedophilia. Culture and society should encourage standards of sexual morality that support and enhance family life.

THE FAMILY AND LIFE

The intrinsic worth, right to life and sanctity of life of every human person exists throughout the continuum of life, from fertilization until natural death.

Every human life is a gift to the person, the family and society. Loving families cherish and serve all their members, including the weak, aged and handicapped. Taking innocent human life through abortion and euthanasia is wrong; respect for human life demands that we choose the life-protecting options of adoption and palliative care. The destruction of embryonic human beings, lethal human embryo experimentation and abortifacients also involve wrongful takings of human life. All experimentation and research on human beings should be beneficial to the particular human subject. Trafficking in the organs and limbs of aborted children and other human beings, cloning humans and human-genetic engineering treat human life as a commodity and should not be allowed. Animal-human genetic experimentation is a crime against humanity. Policy should respect the inherent dignity of human life.

THE FAMILY AND POPULATION

Human society depends on the renewal of the human population; the true population problem is depopulation, not overpopulation. Many nations are experiencing below-replacement fertility, arising from widespread abortion, birth control, lack of interest in marriage and declining family sizes. People are living longer, increasing the size of elderly populations, while there are proportionally decreasing numbers of taxpayers to support their elders' retirement incomes and health care. Because just governments and creative human enterprise and charity offer the best hope for addressing the problems of poverty, hunger and disease, no country should be coerced to accept policies of "population control." Efforts to assist developing countries should focus on promoting family self-sufficiency, not dependency.

THE FAMILY AND EDUCATION

Parents uniquely possess the authority and responsibility to direct the upbringing and education of their children. By its nature, education is not only technical and practical, but also moral and spiritual. The family is the child's first school, parents the first and most important teachers. Love of community and loyalty to nation begin in the family. The state usurps the parental role when it monopolizes and mandates the educational system, and deprives parents of their intrinsic authority over their children's education. Nor should government schools or health clinics treat minor children's health without parental approval.

School curricula should not undermine the right of parents to teach their children moral and spiritual values. Parents have a duty to their children and to society to provide their children an adequate education. Parents should be free to spend their education resources, including tax money, on the schools of their choice, such as sending them to a religious school or educating their children themselves in the home.

THE FAMILY AND THE ECONOMY

Economic policy, both corporate and governmental, should be crafted to allow the family economy to flourish; what is good for families is good for the economy.

Family economy centers on the pursuit of meaningful employment to fulfill one's personal vocation and to provide for the present and future needs, obligations, and desires of the family -- such as food, shelter, education, health care, charity, recreation, retirement income, taxes and the intergenerational family estate.

Healthy families produce good citizens and workers, competent consumers and innovative entrepreneurs. Employers should allow workers flexible family and maternity leave. Corporate philanthropy and national and international funding for economic development should strengthen the natural family. Such funds should not be used to support organizations whose programs harm the family. Commerce in products that appeal to addictions, such as harmful drugs, gambling and violent and pornographic media, undermine the family and should be opposed.

THE FAMILY AND GOVERNMENT

Government should protect and support the family, and not usurp the vital roles it plays in society.

When the state or its agent attempts to exercise a right or responsibility that belongs to the family, albeit with good intentions to address a vexing social problem, its effect is to undermine and displace the family and make matters worse. Government policies should not create pressure for mothers to enter the workplace when they would prefer to care for their families full time. Government should secure an orderly, lawful and just society that allows families freely and responsibly to: form in the covenant of marriage and bear children, pursue meaningful work, provide for their material and health needs, direct the education and upbringing of their children, participate in charitable, civic and recreational activities, care for elderly family members, build estates for their present and future generations, and practice their religion.

THE FAMILY AND RELIGION

Parents have the right to teach their religious and moral beliefs to their children and to raise them according to their religious precepts. Based on, and consistent with, the human right to religious liberty, families have the right to believe, practice and express their religious views in love. Religious institutions should not accommodate cultural trends that undermine the created nature of the family. One need not hold religious views to recognize that the family is part of human nature and the fundamental social unit. Religious institutions have the crucial cultural-leadership role of affirming that: the natural human family is established in creation and is essential to a good society; life and sexuality are gifts from the Creator, to be enjoyed respectfully and wholesomely; the family is sacred and has the unique authority, responsibility and capacity to provide for its members' education, health care and welfare; and all social institutions should respect and uphold the institution of the family.

CALL TO RESPECT THE FAMILY

We exhort all persons, families, social organizations and governments throughout the world to respect and uphold the institution of the natural human family, in accordance with the principles of this Declaration, for the good of present and future generations.

The Mexico City Declaration (2004)

ON THE WORLD CONGRESS OF FAMILIES

The World Congress of Families was initiated by Allan Carlson, President of The Howard Center for Family, Religion and Society. At the first World Congress of Families held in 1997 in Prague, the Czech Republic, a Declaration affirming the central, vital, and essential role of the natural family was adopted. In 1999, the second World Congress of Families adopted a Declaration of Principles about the Family, now called The Geneva Declaration. It called on people of faith and all men and women of good will to work together to strengthen the natural family as the fundamental social unit of society.

We, of the World Congress of Families III, assembled in Mexico City, from many national, ethnic, cultural, academic, social and religious communities, affirm that the natural family is established by the Creator and is fundamental to the good of the society. We also recognize that since the World Congress of Families II, new issues have arisen that threaten the well-being of the family, <u>and</u> marriage, such as euthanasia, reproductive technology, cloning, and other bioethical issues.

OUR PURPOSE

We address ourselves to all people of goodwill who, with the majority of the world's people, value the natural family. Challenges to the family's very legitimacy as an institution include extreme individualism, easy divorce, radical homosexual activisim, irresponsible sexual behavior, and the reinterpretation and misapplication of human rights. To protect and promote the family and to direct public policy with a family perspective, this Declaration asserts principles and recommends actions that respect and uphold the vital functions that the family plays in society.

THE FAMILY AND SOCIETY

Principle

The natural family is the fundamental social unit, inscribed in human nature, and centered on the union of a man and a woman in the lifelong covenant of marriage. The natural family is defined by marriage, including extended family members, procreation, and adoption. Secure and stable families that welcome children are necessary for a healthy society.

Actions

• Encourage governments to uphold and maintain the natural understanding of marriage.

- Provide special benefits to the unique relationship of man and woman in marriage.

- Recognize that the security of nations and the survival of civilization depend upon the strength of families worldwide.

- Establish an effective information system to compile and disseminate information on family friendly policies.

- Promote research on family issues through specialized institutions.

- Encourage media and other institutions (such as schools and non-governmental organizations) to uphold the above principle.

THE FAMILY AND MARRIAGE

Principle

Marriage, the cornerstone of healthy family life, brings security, contentment, meaning, joy and spiritual maturity to the man and woman who enter this lifelong covenant with unselfish commitment. In marriage, both husband and wife commit to a life of mutual love, respect, support and compassion. Steadfast commitment in marriage provides the security in family life that is needed by children. Children are entitled to the complementary parental love and attention of both father and mother, which marriage bestows. Due to the importance of a child being raised by a mother and a father, social policies should not encourage cohabitation or single parenting.

Actions

- Present marriage as a desirable good for men and women.

- Implement programs to prepare men and women for marriage in order to increase their chances of success.

- Promote measures that aid in the healing of troubled marriages and broken homes.

- Revise laws to encourage commitment to the marriage relationship.

- Take legal or other appropriate action in cases of abusive relationships.

- Encourage media and other institutions (such as schools and non-governmental organizations) to uphold the above principle.

THE FAMILY AND CHILDREN

Principle

The natural family provides the optimal environment for the healthy development of children. Healthy family life fulfills the basic human need to belong and satisfies the longings of the human heart to give and receive love. The family shapes the human person's attitude towards such fundamental matters as identity, security, responsibility, love, morality, and religion. In personal and intimate ways, the natural family cares for its children and provides for their spiritual, physical, intellectual, social, psychological, and ethical growth.

Actions

- Encourage and support mothers in their essential role in caring for their children.

- Recognize the vital role of fathers in child rearing.

- Facilitate adoptions as a means to provide children with a family and to reduce abortions.

- Recognize the right of all children to a father <u>and</u> a mother.

- Support agencies which assist women and families in crisis.

- Strive for a society where all families have access to good homes, health care, and nourishment and opportunities for physical, intellectual and recreational development.

- Encourage media and other institutions (such as schools and non-governmental organizations) to uphold the above principle.

THE FAMILY AND SEXUALITY

Principle

Sexuality exists for the expression of love between husband and wife and for the procreation of children in the covenant of marriage. Marriage between a man and a woman forms the moral context for sexual union. The complementary natures of men and women, both physically and psychologically, are evident throughout the course of human history and in every society. Deviations from natural sexual behavior cannot truly satisfy the human spirit. Culture, society, and government should encourage standards of sexual morality that support and enhance family life.

Actions

- Give unique recognition to the societal benefits of the complementary relationship of man and woman in marriage.

- Take appropriate actions to assist homosexuals in programs of voluntary rehabilitation.

- Encourage media and other institutions (such as schools and non-governmental organizations) to recognize and encourage the unique importance of traditional marriage.

THE FAMILY, LIFE, AND BIOETHICAL ISSUES

Principle

Every human person has intrinsic value throughout the continuum of life from fertilization until natural death. Every human life is a gift to the person, the family and society. Loving families cherish and serve all their members, including the weak, aged and handicapped. Taking innocent human life through abortion and euthanasia is a direct attack on human life and dignity. Respect for human life demands the life-protecting options of adoption and palliative care. The destruction of embryonic human beings, lethal human embryo experimentation and abortifacients also involve the wrongful taking of human life.

Actions

- Protect and respect through public policy the inherent dignity of human life.

- Prohibit by law all forms of artificial manipulation of human life that threaten human dignity, including cloning, in vitro fertilization, abortion, and embryo experimentation.

- Encourage media and other institutions (such as schools and non-governmental organizations) to uphold the above principle.

THE FAMILY AND POPULATION

Principle

Procreation is the key to the survival of the human race. An increasing number of countries are experiencing below replacement birth rates due to misguided population-control programs that promote contraception, abortion, delayed marriages, and the abandonment of the institution of marriage. Demographic growth is an indication of the expansion of human resources that represents challenges and opportunities, not burdens (poverty, hunger, and disease have other causes, including a lack of good will and misuse of governmental resources). These problems can be solved by education, creative social policies, economic development and promotion of family integrity regardless of geographical boundaries, cultural practices and religious affiliation.

Actions

• Make individuals aware of the positive social consequences of parenthood within marriage.

• Provide incentives by the state and educational institutions to promote marriage and support the natural family and pro-life policies aimed at reversing the declining fertility rate.

• In countries with below replacement birthrates, encourage an increase in population to provide a broad foundation to help support the expanded elderly population.

• Allocate public resources to encourage responsible married-couple families to have children.

- Craft an economic system that allows women to stay home and to bear the number of children they desire.

- Affirm that environmental improvement can be compatible with population growth.

- Encourage media and other institutions (such as schools and non-governmental organizations) to uphold the above principle.

THE FAMILY AND EDUCATION

Principle

Parents possess the primary authority and responsibility to direct the upbringing and education of their children, except in clear cases of abuse and neglect. By its nature, education is not only technical and practical but also moral and spiritual. The family is the child's first school with parents their first and most important teachers. The state usurps the parental role when it monopolizes and mandates the educational system and deprives parents of their intrinsic authority over their children's education. School curricula should not undermine the right of parents to teach their children moral and spiritual values. Parents have a duty to their children and to society to provide their children an adequate education. Parents should be free to spend their resources for education, including tax money, on the schools of their choice, such as sending them to a religious school or educating their children themselves in the home.

Actions

- Structure state policy to respect the natural authority and primary responsibility of parents over the education of their children.

- Craft policies that are responsive to parents who need assistance in fulfilling this duty.

- Encourage media and other institutions (such as schools and non-governmental organizations) to uphold the above principle.

THE FAMILY, ECONOMY AND DEVELOPMENT

Principle

The natural family is the fundamental unit in society for economic growth and development. Promoting the dignity of families and respecting their rights are necessary conditions for a healthy and stable society. A nation cannot create true wealth if its policies lead to family disintegration. Policies that promote responsible government, sustain economic growth, care for the environment, and promote cultural harmony must also support the family. The advancement of economic, social, technological and political growth is necessary, but not sufficient for, true human development.

Actions

- Formulate and implement public programs which include the family perspective within all government entities.

- Require evaluations of the impact of public policies on the natural family.

- Empower families to break the cycle of poverty.

- Include the health and stability of the family as an indicator of development.

- Facilitate work conditions that allow both men and women to fulfill their respective family responsibilities.

- Encourage media and other institutions (such as schools and non-governmental organizations) to uphold the above principle.

THE FAMILY AND GOVERNMENT

Principle

Government should protect and support the natural family and not usurp the vital roles that it plays in society. Government policies should not create pressure for mothers to enter the workplace when they would prefer to care for their families full time. Government should secure an orderly, lawful, and just society that allows families freely and responsibly to:

- Marry and bear children
- Pursue meaningful work
- Provide for their material and health needs
- Direct the education and upbringing of their children
- Participate in charitable, civic and recreational activities
- Care for elderly family members
- Provide security for their present and future generations, and
- Practice their religion.

Actions

- Formulate public policies that allow mothers the choice to remain at home and care for their children.

- Make the health of the family the primary focus of international agencies.

- Encourage international agencies to embrace the family perspective.

- Re-examine international laws and policies that may harm the well-being of the natural family.

- Encourage Heads of State and other high governmental officials to issue proclamations affirming the natural family.

- Identify or create international mechanisms to foster cooperation in the interests of the natural family.

- Promote public policies with a clear family perspective.

- Encourage the media and other institutions (such as schools and non-governmental organizations) to uphold the above principle.

THE FAMILY AND RELIGION

Principle

As the primary educators, parents have the right to teach their religious and moral beliefs to their children and to raise them according to their religious precepts. Based on and consistent with the human right to religious liberty, families have the right to believe, practice and express their religious views. Religious institutions should not accommodate cultural trends that undermine the created nature of the family. Religious institutions have the crucial cultural-leadership role of affirming that:

- The natural human family is established in creation
- The family is essential to a good society, and

- Life and sexuality are gifts from the creator to be enjoyed, respectfully and wholesomely.

Actions

- Recognize that the state, its agencies, the media or other entities should not undermine the parents' role in teaching their children a belief system and raising them accordingly.

- Encourage media and other institutions (such as schools and non-governmental organizations) to uphold the above principle.

CALL TO RESPECT THE FAMILY

We exhort all persons, families, social entities, governments, and international organizations throughout the world to adopt the family perspective to craft and pursue realistic targets for action, and to respect and uphold the institution of the natural human family for the good of present and future generations, in accordance with the principles and recommended guidelines of the Declaration adopted at the third World Congress of Families in Mexico City.

Adopted March 31, 2004, Mexico City, Mexico

Notes

Introduction

1   http://www.unmarriedamerica.org/column-one/3-6-06-natural-family-resolu-tion.htm (7/7/06).
2   http://www.pamspaulding.com/weblog/2005/03/natural-family-vs-homo-agen-da.html (7/7/06).
3   http://www.salon.com/politics/war_room/?blogs/politics/war_room/2005/03/17/family/index.html (4/4/05).
4   http://www.whatsupwithkanab.com/blog (7/7/06); "Utah Town's Pro-Family Resolution Sparks Debate," at: www.gopusa.com/news/2006/february/0228_utah_marriageep.shtml (7/7/06).

The Natural Family· A Manifesto

1   Theodore Roosevelt, *Presidential Addresses and State Papers of Theodore Roosevelt. Part Two* (New York: P.F. Collier & Son, [1904?]): 493.
2   Francis Fukuyama, *The Great Disruption: Human Nature and the Reconstruction of Social Order* (New York: Free Press, 1999).
3   Karl Polanyi, *The Great Transformation* (New York: Rinehart & Company, 1944).
4   John C. Caldwell, *Theory of Fertility Decline* (London & New York: Academic Press, 1982): 324.
5   For example: Thomas Hobbes, *De Cive: The English Version* [1642] (Oxford: Clarendon Press, 1983): 42-48, 122-24.

228

6   As example: Jean Jacques Rousseau, *The Social Contract* [1762] (New York: E.P. Dutton, 1950).

7   Louis deBonald, *On Divorce* [1801], trans. and edited by Nicholas Davidson (New Brunswick, NJ: Transaction, 1992).

8   Edmund Burke, *Reflections on the Revolution in France* (London: J. Dodsley, 1790).

9   G.K. Chesterton, *What's Wrong With the World* [1910] and *The Superstition of Divorce* [1920]; in *Collected Works*. Volume IV (San Francisco: Ignatius Press, 1987): 67, 256.

10 Phillip Longman, *The Empty Cradle: How Falling Birthrates Threaten World Prosperity and What to Do About It* (New York: Basic Books, 2004).

11 Phrases borrowed from David Schindler, The John Paul II Institute, Washington, DC.

12 Jan Lewis, *The Pursuit of Happiness: Family and Values in Jefferson's Virginia* (Cambridge, UK: Cambridge University Press, 1985); and Barry Alan Shain, *The Myth of American Individualism: The Protestant Origins of American Political Thought* (Princeton, NJ: Princeton University Press, 1996).

13 Daniel Patrick Moynihan, *The Negro Family: The Case for National Action* [1965]; in Lee Rainwater and William L. Yancey, eds., *The Moynihan Report and The Politics of Controversy* (Cambridge, MA: M.I.T. Press, 1967).

14 *The Universal Declaration of Human Rights* (Adopted and Proclaimed by the General Assembly of The United Nations, 10 December 1948): Articles 16(3), 25(1 and 2), 26.

15 See the research abstracts available through "New Research" at SwanSearch (www.profam.org); also, the Family and Society Database at www.heritage. org.

16 C. Owen Lovejoy, "The Origin of Man," *Science* 211 (Jan. 23, 1981): 348.

17 Carle C. Zimmerman, *Family and Civilization* (New York & London: Harper & Brothers, 1947).

1   *A School of Despotism?*

1   From a statement submitted to authors, April 2005.

2   Thomas Hobbes, *DeCive: The English Version* (Oxford: Clarendon Press, 1983): 42-48, 122-24.

3   John Locke, *Of Civil Government (Second Essay)* (Ann Arbor, MI: Edwards Brothers, 1947): 35-37, 41-44, 51-54.

4   John Stuart Mill, *The Subjection of Women* (Cambridge, MA: The MIT Press, 1970): 22, 28-29, 36-37, 48.

5   John Rawls, *A Theory of Justice* (Cambridge, MA: The Belknap Press of Harvard University, 1971): 74, 301, 462-63, 511.

6   John Jacques Rousseau, *The Social Contract* (New York: E. Dutton, 1950): 44, 15, 27; and an extract from Rousseau's *The Government of Poland*, found in Philip Abbott, *The Family on Trial: Special Relationships in Modern Political Thought* (State College, PA: The Pennsylvania State University Press, 1981): 55-56.

7   Arthur W. Calhoun, *A Social History of the American Family* (New York: Barnes & Noble, 1945 [1918]): 171-72.

8   Claudia Koonz, *Mothers in the Fatherland: Women, the Family, and Nazi Politics* (New York: St. Marten's Press, 1987): 178.

9   Koonz, *Mothers in the Fatherland*, p. 398.

10   Friedrich Engels, *The Origin of the Family, Private Property and the State* (Chicago: Charles H. Kerr & Co., 1902 [1884]).

11   A Woman Resident in Russia, "The Russian Effort to Abolish Marriage," *The Atlantic* (July 1926), p. 1; at http:www.theatlantic.com/cgi-bin/send.cgi?page=http%3A//www.theatlantic.com/issues/2 (6/2/2004).

12   Alexandra Kollontai, "Communism and the Family," *Komunistka* (No. 2, 1920): 8, 10; at http://www.marxists.org/archive/kollontai/works/1920/communism-family.htm (6/2/2004).

13   Barry Levy, "'Tender Plants': Quaker Farmers and Children in the Delaware Valley, 1681-1735," *Journal of Family History* 3 (Summer 1978): 117.

14   James A. Henretta, "Families and Farms: Mentalite in Pre-Industrial America," *William and Mary Quarterly* 35 (Jan. 1978): 20-21.

15   Jan Lewis, *The Pursuit of Happiness: Family and Values in Jefferson's Virginia* (Cambridge, England: Cambridge University Press, 1983): 204-05.

16   See: Allan Carlson, *The 'American Way': Family and Community in the Shaping of the American Identity* (Wilmington, DE: ISI Books, 2003).

17   Barry Alan Shain, *The Myth of American Individualism* (Princeton, NJ: Princeton University Press, 1994).

18   Hugh Brody, "Nomads and Settlers," in Anthony Barnett and Roger Scruton, eds., *Town and Country* (London: Vintage, 1999): 3-4.

19   G.K. Chesterton, *The Superstition of Divorce*; in *Collected Works*, Vol. IV, *Family, Society, Politics* (San Francisco: Ignatius Press, 1987): 259-60.

20   See Karl Polanyi, *The Great Transformation* (New York: Farrar & Rinehart, 1944).

21   Robert Nisbet, *The Quest for Community: A Study in the Ethics of Order & Freedom* (San Francisco: Institute for Contemporary Studies, 1990 [1953]): 247, 257.

22   John C. Caldwell and Thomas Schindlmeyer, "Explanations of the Fertility Crisis in Modern Societies: A Search for Commonalities," *Population Studies* 57 (2003): 241-63.

23   *Two Basic Social Encyclicals* (Washington, DC: The Catholic University of American Press, 1943): 5-11, 15, 55-59, 133-35.

24   See: Hubert Curtis Callahan, S.J., *The Family Allowance Procedure: An Analysis*

of the Family Allowance Procedure in Selected Countries (Washington, DC: The Catholic University of America Press, 1947): 3, 68.

25 Quoted in Molly Ladd-Taylor, *Mother-Work: Women, Child Welfare, and the State, 1890-1930* (Urbana: University of Illinois Press, 1994): 91. Emphasis added.

26 On the arguably "pro-family" nature of the New Deal, see: Allan Carlson, *The 'American Way', 55-78.*

27 Evidence for the direct positive effects of these innovations on family formation can be found in: Harvey S. Rosen, "Owner Occupied Housing and the Federal Income Tax: Estimates and Simulations," *Journal of Urban Economics* 6 (1979): 263-64; D. Laidler, "Income Tax Incentives for Owner-Occupied Housing," in A.C. Harberger and M.J. Bailey, eds., *The Taxation of Income from Capital* (Washington, DC: The Brookings Institution, 1969): 50-64; Leslie Whittington, "Taxes and the Family: The Impact of the Tax Exemption for Dependents on Marital Fertility," *Demography* 29 (May 1992): 220-22; and L.A. Whittington, J. Alms, and H.E. Peters, "Fertility and the Personal Exemption: Implicit Pronatalist Policy in the United States," *The American Economic Review* 80 (June 1990): 545-56.

28 Alva Myrdal, "Kollektiv bostadsform," *Tiden* 24 (Dec. 1932): 602; Alva Myrdal, "Yrkes-kvinnansbarn," *Yrkes-kvinnor klubbnytt* (Feb. 1933): 63; Alva Myrdal, *Stadsbarn: En boken deres föstran i storbarnkammare* (Stockholm: Koopertiva förbundets bökförlag, 1935); and Alva and Gunnar Myrdal, *Kris i befolkningsfrågan* (Stockholm: Bonniers, 1934).

2 *A Bulwark of Liberty*

1 Genesis 1: 27-28; 2: 24 (Revised Standard Version).

2 John D. Lierman, "The Family and the Word," *The Religion & Society Report* 22 (June 2005): 9.

3 Edward Westermarck, *The History of Human Marriage: 5th Edition* (London: Macmillan, 1925): 26-37, 69-72.

4 George Peter Murdock, *Social Structure* (New York: The Free Press, 1965 [1949]): 1-8.

5 C. Owen Lovejoy, "The Origin of Man," *Science* 211 (Jan. 23, 1981): 348. Emphasis added.

6 Ronald S. Immerman, "Perspectives on Human Attachment (Pair Bonding): Eve's Unique Legacy of a Canine Analogue," *Evolutionary Psychology* 1 (2003): 138-54.

7 Phillip L. Reno, Richard S. Meindl, Melanie A. McCollum, and C. Owen Lovejoy, "Sexual Dimorphism in Australopithecus afarensis was similar to modern humans," *Proceedings of the National Academy of Science* 100 (Aug. 5, 2003): 9404-09.

8   For the seminal work, see: Pierre Guillaume and Frederic LePlay, *Le Reform Sociale*, Vol. 1, Book 3 (Tours: A Mame et fils, 1887): chapters 24-30.

9   See: Carle Zimmerman and Pitirim Sorokin, *Principles of Rural-Urban Sociology* (New York: Henry Holt and Co., 1929).

10   Carle Zimmerman and Merle Frampton, *Family and Society: A Study of Sociological Reconstruction* (New York: D. Van Nostrand, 1935): 133, 221-37.

11   See: Pitirim Sorokin, *The Crisis of Our Age* (New York: E.P. Dutton, 1941); also Pitirim Sorokin, *The American Sex Revolution* (Boston: Porter Sargeant, 1956).

12   Robert Nisbet, *Quest for Community: A Study in the Ethics of Order & Freedom* (San Francisco: Institute for Contemporary Studies, 1990 [1953]); and Robert Nisbet, *Twilight of Authority* (New York: Oxford University Press, 1975).

13   Nisbet, *Twilight of Authority*, p. 254.

14   Ibid., p. 260.

15   C.S. Lewis, *The Screwtape Letters* (New York: Harper San Francisco, 1942): 53-54. Emphasis added.

16   Martin Luther, *Luther's Works. Vol. 5: Lectures on Genesis. Chapters 1-5* (St. Louis: Concordia, 1958): 133.

17   *Luther's Works. Vol. 5*, 133.

18   Emile Durkheim, *Suicide: A Study in Sociology*, trans. John A. Spaulding and George Simpson (Glencoe, IL: The Free Press of Glencoe, 1951).

19   Martin E.P. Seligman, *Authentic Happiness* (New York: Free Press, 2002): 55-56.

20   For example, see: Myriam Khlat, Catherine Sermet, and Annick LePape, "Women's Health in Relation with their Family and Work Roles: France from the early 1990s," *Social Science and Medicine* 50 (2000): 1807-25.

21   Nicholas Eberstadt, "Power and Population in Asia," *Policy Review Online* (Feb. 2004); at http:www.policyreview.org/Feb04/eberstadt.html (6/10/05).

22   Phillip Longman, *The Empty Cradle: How Falling Birthrates Threaten World Prosperity [And What to Do About It]* (New York: Basic Books, 2004): 11.

23   Donald Critchlow, *Intended Consequences: Birth Control, Abortion and the Federal Government in Modern America* (New York: Oxford University Press, 1999).

24   Joan Huber, "Will U.S. Fertility Decline Toward Zero?" *The Sociological Quarterly* 21 (Autumn 1980): 481-92.

25   Ron Lesthaeghe, "A Century of Demographic and Cultural Change in Western Europe," *Population and Development Review* 9 (1983): 411-35.

26   Dirk Van de Kaa, *Europe's Second Demographic Transition* (Washington, DC: Population Reference Bureau, 1987): 25.

27   Philippe Aries, "Two Successive Motivations for the Declining Birth Rate in the West," *Population and Development Review* 6 (Dec. 1980): 649-50.

28   John C. Caldwell, *Theory of Fertility Decline* (London and New York: Academic Press, 1982): 324.

29 G.K. Chesterton, *Collected Works: Volume IV: Family, Society, Politics* (San Francisco: Ignatius Press, 1987): 256.

30 Chesterton, *Collected Works, IV*, pp. 67-68.

31 Yvonne Hirdman, "the Importance of Gender in the Swedish Labor Movement, Or: A Swedish Dilemma," paper prepared for The Swedish National Institute of Working Life," 2002, pp. 3-5, 10; and Frances Fox Piven "Ideology and the State: Women, Power and the Welfare State," in Linda Gordon, ed., *Women, the State and Welfare* (Madison, WI: University of Wisconsin Press, 1990): 251-64.

32 Claudia Koonz, *Mothers in the Fatherland: Women, the Family, and Nazi Politics* (New York: St. Martin's Press, 1987): 393.

33 Marfua Toktakhodjaeva, "Society and Family in Uzbekistan," *Polish Sociological Reviewi* 2 (1997): 149-165.

34 Li Zong, "Agricultural Reform and Its Impact on Chinese Rural Families, 1978-1989," *Journal of Comparative Family Studies* 24 (Autumn 1993).

35 H. Ruigrok, J. Dronkers, B. Mach, "Communism and the Decline of the Family: Resemblance between the occupational levels of Polish siblings from different gender, generations, political background and family forms." Paper presented at the Seventh Social Science Study Day conference, April 11-12, 1996, The University of Amsterdam.

36 *Illustrated London News*, June 17, 1933.

37 In Mario Einaudi and Francois Goguel, *Christian Democracy in Italy and France* (Notre Dame, IN: University of Notre Dame Press, 1952): 126.

38 Guido Dierick, "Christian Democracy and Its Ideological Rivals: An Empirical Comparison in the Low Countries," in David Hanley, ed., *Christian Democracy in Europe: A Comparative Perspective* (London & New York: Pinter Publishers, 1994): 24.

39 R.E.M. Irving, *Christian Democracy in France* (London: George Allen & Unwin, 1973): 61-62.

40 Noel D. Cary, *The Path to Christian Democracy: German Catholics and the Party System from Windthorst to Adenauer* (Cambridge, MA: Harvard University Press, 1996): 180.

41 From: Johannes Morsink, *The Universal Declaration of Human Rights: Origins, Drafting, and Intent* (Philadelphia: University of Pennsylvania Press, 1999): 255.

42 Morsink, *The Universal Declaration of Human Rights*, p. 255.

3 The Fundamental Unit of Society

1   The Howard Center for Family, Religion & Society, "Special Report: Results of a Global Survey on Marriage and the Family." Prepared by Wirthlin Worldwide (November 1999). Some responded with two choices; hence the numbers total over 100 percent.

2   The authors recognize that in the United States and a number of other countries, non-profit corporations exist.

3   *Dartmouth* v. *Woodward* (1819).

4   *Eternal Truths and the Sciences*

1   Arthur W. Calhoun, *A Social History of the American Family: From Colonial Times to the Present* (New York: Barnes & Noble, 1945 [1917]): 165-75.

2   Gunnar Myrdal, "Social politikens dilemma," *Spektrum* 2 (No. 3, 1932): 1-13; and (No. 4, 1932): 13-31.

3   Robert Nisbet, *The Sociological Tradition* (New York: Basic Books, 1966): 11, 17.

4   John Devereux and Luis Locay, "Specialization, Household Production, and the Measurement of Economic Growth," *The American Economic Review* 82 (1992): 399-403. Reuben Gronau, "Home Production—A Forgotten Industry," *The Review of Economics and Statistics* 62 (1980): 408-416. Edward P. Lazear and Robert T. Michael, "Real Income Equivalence Among One-Earner and Two-Earner Families," *The American Economic Review* 70 (1980): 203-208. Duncan Ironmonger, "The Domestic Economy: $340 Billion of G.H.P.," in *The Family: There is No Other Way* (Melbourne: Australian Family Association, 1996): 132-146.

5   T.R. Balakrishnan et al., "A Hazard Model Analysis of the Covariates of Marriage Dissolution in Canada," *Demography* 24 (1987): 398-400; Erik E. Filsinger and Margaret R. Wilson, "Religiosity and Marital Adjustment: Multidimensional Interrelationships," *Journal of Marriage and the Family* 48 (1986): 147-151.

6   Erik E. Filsinger, "Religiosity, Socioeconomic Rewards, and Family Development: Predictors of Marital Adjustment," *Journal of Marriage and the Family* 46 (1984): 663-670; Richard A. Hunt and Morton R. King, "Religiosity and Marriage," *Journal for the Scientific Study of Religion* 17 (1978): 399-406. Leon R. Kass, *The Beginning of Wisdom: Reading Genesis* (New York: Free Press, 2003), 119-121. Maria Krysan, Kristin A. Moore, and Nicholas Zill, "Research on Families," Report on a Conference Convened by the Office of the Assistant Secretary for Planning and Evaluation, U.S. Department of Health and Human Services, 10 May 1990.

7   Robert A. Aldrich and Glenn Austin, *Grandparenting for the 90's* (Incline Village: Robert Erdmann, 1991): 15-20. Arthur Kornhaber, "Grandparenthood and the 'New Social Contract,'" in *Grandparenthood*, ed. Vern L. Bengston and Joan F. Robertson (Beverly Hills: Sage, 1985): 160-165. Thomas E. Denham and Craig W. Smith, "The Influence of Grandparents on Grandchildren: A Review of the Literature and Resources," *Family Relations* 38 (1989): 340-345.

8   Allan C. Carlson, *From Cottage to Work Station: The Family's Search for Social Harmony in the Industrial Age* (San Francisco: Ignatius, 1993). John Devereux and Luis Locay, "Specialization, Household Production, and the Measurement

of Economic Growth," *The American Economic Review* 82 (1992): 399-403. Stuart Ewen, *Captains of Consciousness: Advertising and the Social Roots of the Consumer Culture* (New York: McGraw Hill, 1976): 161-164. Paul C. Glick, "The Family Life Cycle and Social Change," *Family Relations* 38 (1989): 123-189.

9   Glenna Matthews, *'Just a Housewife': The Rise and Fall of Domesticity in America* (New York: Oxford, 1987): 146-171. Karl Polanyi, *The Great Transformation* (New York: Rinehart, 1943), 74-75, 83, 92. Pitirim Sorokin, *Social and Cultural Dynamics: A Study of Change in Major Systems of Art, Truth, Ethics, Law, and Social Relationships*, rev. and abridged ed. (1957; rpt. New Brunswick: Transaction, 1985): 695-705.

10 Duane Quiatt and Jack Kelso, "Household Economics and Hominid Origins," *Current Anthropology* 26 (1985): 207-211. Joel R. Peck and Marcus W. Feldman, "Kin Selection and the Evolution of Monogamy," *Science* 240 (1988): 1672-1674.

11 American Academy of Pediatrics Task Force on the Family, "Family Pediatrics," *Pediatrics* 111 Supplement (2003): 1541-1553. Susan L. Brown, "Family Structure and Child Well-Being: The Significance of Parental Cohabitation," *Journal of Marriage and Family* 66 (2004): 351-367.

12 Cheryl Buehler and Kay Pasley, "Family Boundary Ambiguity, Marital Status and Child Adjustment," *Journal of Early Adolescence* 20 (2000): 281-308.

13 David H. Demo and Alan C. Acock, "Family Structure, Family Process, and Adolescent Well-Being," *Journal of Research on Adolescence* 6 (1996): 457-488. Stephen Demuth and Susan L. Brown, "Family Structure, Family Processes, and Adolescent Delinquency: The Significance of Parental Absence Versus Parental Gender," *Journal of Research in Crime and Delinquency* 41 (2004): 58-81.

14 Toni Richards et al., "Changing Living Arrangements: A Hazard Model of Transitions Among Household Types," *Demography* 24 (1987): 77-85.

15 Wendy D. Manning and Kathleen A. Lamb, "Adolescent Well-Being in Cohabiting, Married, and Single-Parent Families," *Journal of Marriage and Family* 65 (2003): 876-893.

16 Karen F. Parker and Tracy Johns, "Urban Disadvantage and Types of Race-Specific Homicide: Assessing the Diversity in Family Structures in the Urban Context," *Journal of Research in Crime and Delinquency* 39 (2002): 277-303.

17 Ronald S. Immerman and Wade C. Mackey, "The Societal Dilemma of Multiple Sexual Partners: The Costs of the Loss of Pair-Bonding," *Marriage and Family Review* 29 (1999): 3-14.

18 Randal D. Day and Wade C. Mackey, "Children as Resources: A Cultural Analysis," *Family Perspective* 20 (1985): 258-262. Jon Elvind Kolberg, "The Gender Dimension of the Welfare State," *International Journal of Sociology* 21 (1991): 119-146.

19 Jennifer Roback Morse, *Love & Economics: Why the Laissez-Faire Family Doesn't Work* (Dallas: Spence, 2001), 89-136. Natalie Rogoff Ramsøy, "Non-marital Co-

habitation and Change in Norms: The Case of Norway," *Acta Sociologica* 37 (1994): 23-27.

20   Frances D'Souza, "Democracy as a Cure for Famine," *Journal of Peace Research* 31 (1994): 369-373. Ann Gibbons, "Famine: Blame Policy, not Nature," *Science* 254 (1991): 790.

21   Barbara Jancar, "Democracy and the Environment in Eastern Europe and the Soviet Union," *Harvard International Review* 12.4 (1990): 13-18. Martin Ravillion, "Famines and Economics," *Journal of Economic Literature* 35 (1997): 1205-1247.

22   Julian Simon, "The Effects of Population on Nutrition and Economic Well-Being," *Journal of Interdisciplinary History* 14 (1983): 413-437. Julian Simon, *The Ultimate Resource* (Princeton: Princeton University Press, 1981). Julian Simon, *The Ultimate Resource* 2 (Princeton: Princeton University Press, 1996).

23   Anatoly I. Antonov, "Depopulation and Family Failure in Russia," *The Family in America* 15 (July 2001): 1-8. John C. Caldwell, "Demographic Theory: The Long View," *Population and Development Review* 30 (2004): 297-316. John C. Caldwell and Thomas Schindlmayr, "Explanations of the fertility crisis in modern societies: A search for commonalities," *Population Studies* 57 (2003): 241-263. Philip Longman, *How Falling Birthrates Threaten World Prosperity and What to Do About It* (New York: Basic, 2004).

24   Shawn L Christiansen and Rob Palkovitz, "Why the 'Good Provider' Role Still Matters," *Journal of Family Issues* 22 (2001): 84-106. Mohammadreza Hojat, "Satisfaction with Early Relationships with Parents and Psychosocial Attributes in Adulthood: Which Parent Contributes More?" *The Journal of Genetic Psychology* 159 (1998): 202-220. Myriam Khlat, Catherine Sermet, and Annick Le Pape, "Women's health in relation with their family and work roles: France in the early 1990s," *Social Science & Medicine* 50 (2000): 1807-1825.

25   Robert M. Orrange, "Individualism, Family Values, and the Professional Middle Class: In-Depth Interviews with Advanced Law and MBA Students," *The Sociological Quarterly* 44 (2003): 451-480. Arland Thornton and Linda Young-DeMarco, "Four Decades of Trends in Attitudes Toward Family Issues in the United States: The 1960's Through the 1990's," *Journal of Marriage and the Family* 63 (2001): 1009-1037. Lynn Y. Weiner, "Reconstructing Motherhood: The La Leche League in Postwar America," *The Journal of American History* 80 (1994): 1357-1381.

26   Gary Becker, "A Theory of Marriage: Part I," *The Journal of Political Economy* 81 (1973): 813-846. Kass, *The Beginning of Wisdom*, 119-121.

27   David M. Buss, "Sex Differences in Human Mate Preferences: Evolutionary Hypotheses Tested in 37 Cultures," *Behavioral and Brain Sciences* 12 (1989): 1-14. Maryann Davis and Eugene Emory, "Sex Differences in Neonatal Stress Reactivity," *Child Development* 66 (1995): 14-27. Christine De Lacoste-Utamsing and Ralph L. Holloway, "Sexual Dimorphism in the Human Corpus Callosum," *Science* 216 (1982): 1431-1432.

28   Alice H. Eagley, "The Science and Politics of Comparing Men and Women," *American Psychologist* 50 (1995): 145-158. Doreen Kimura, "Sex Differences in the Brain," *Scientific American* (August 1992): 32-37.

29   Lloyd B. Lueptow, Lori Garovich-Szabo, and Margaret B. Lueptow, "Social Change and the Persistence of Sex Typing 1974-1997," *Social Forces* 80 (2001): 1-35. Jennifer W. Makin and Richard H. Porter, "Attractiveness of Lactating Females' Breast Odors to Neonates," *Child Development* 60 (1989): 803-810. Virginia A. Mann et al., "Sex Differences in Cognitive Abilities: A Cross-Cultural Perspective," *Neuropsychologia* 28 (1990): 1063-1077.

30   Linda Mealey, *Sex Differences: Developmental and Evolutionary Strategies* (San Diego: Academic Press, 2000): 11-23, 376-377. Irwin Silverman and Marion Eals, "Sex Differences in Spatial Abilities: Evolutionary Theory and Data," in *The Adapted Mind: Evolutionary Psychology and the Generation of Culture* (New York: Oxford University Press, 1992): 533-579. Martin Van Creveld, "A Woman's Place: Reflections on the Origin of Violence," *Social Order* 76 (2000): 825-846. J. Richard Udry, "Biological Limits of Gender Construction," *American Sociological Review* 65 (2000): 443-457.

31   Martin Van Creveld, "A Woman's Place: Reflections on the Origin of Violence," *Social Order* 76 (2000): 825-846. J. Richard Udry, "Biological Limits of Gender Construction," *American Sociological Review* 65 (2000): 443-457.

32   Gary Becker, "A Theory of Marriage: Part I," *The Journal of Political Economy* 81 (1973): 813-846. Gary Becker, "A Theory of Marriage: Part II," *The Journal of Political Economy* 82 (1974): S11-S26. Sanders D. Korenman and David Neumark, "Does Marriage Really Make Men More Productive?" No. 29 in the Finance and Economics Discussion Series, Division of Research and Statistics, Federal Reserve Board, May 1988.

33   Karin L. Brewster et al., "The Changing Impact of Religion on the Sexual and Contraceptive Behavior of Adolescent Women in the United States," *Journal of Marriage and Family* 60 (1998): 493-503. Niclas Berggren, "Rhetoric or Reality? An Economic Analysis of the Effects of Religion in Sweden," *Journal of Socio-Economics* 26 (1997): 571-596. Robert H. DuRant, Robert Pendergast, and Carolyn Seymore, "Sexual Behavior Among Hispanic Female Adolescents in the United States," *Pediatrics* 85 (1990): 1051-1058.

34   Day and Mackey, "Children as Resources: A Cultural Analysis," 258-262. Mark A. Fossett and K. Jill Kiecolt, "Mate Availability and Family Structure among African Americans in U.S. Metropolitan Areas," *Journal of Marriage and the Family* 55 (1993): 288-302.

35   Diane K. McLaughlin and Daniel T. Lichter, "Poverty and the Marital Behavior of Young Women," *Journal of Marriage and the Family* 59 (1997): 582-594.

36   Charles Murray, "Does Welfare Bring More Babies?" *Public Interest* No. 115 (1994): 17-30. David T. Ellwood, "Anti-Poverty Policy for Families in the Next

Century: From Welfare to Work—and Worries," *The Journal of Economic Perspectives* 14 (2002): 187-198. Daniel Lichter and Rukamalie Jayakody, "Welfare Reform: How Do We Measure Success?" *Annual Review of Sociology* 28 (2002): 117- 142.

37   Douglas W. Allen, "Marriage and Divorce: Comment," *The American Economic Review* 82 (1992): 679-685. Leora Friedberg, "Did Unilateral Divorce Raise Divorce Rates? Evidence from Panel Data," *The American Economic Review* 88 (1998): 608-627. Thomas B. Marvell, "Divorce Rates and the Fault Requirement," *Law and Society Review* 23 (1989): 544-563.

38   Paul A. Nakonezny, Robert D. Shull, and Joseph Lee Rodgers, "The Effect of No-Fault Divorce Law on the Divorce Rate Across the 50 States and Its Relation to Income, Education, and Religiosity," *Journal of Marriage and the Family* 57 (1995): 477-488.

39   Lynn D. Wardle, "No-Fault Divorce and the Divorce Conundrum," *Brigham Young University Law Review* 13 (1991): 79-142. Lenore J. Weitzman, "The Divorce Law Revolution and the Transformation of Legal Marriage," in *Contemporary Marriage: Comparative Perspectives on a Changing Institution*, ed. Kingsley Davis (New York: Russell Sage, 1985): 305-335.

5   *Life, Death, Work, and Taxes*

1   Kenneth S. Abraham, "Efficiency and Fairness In Insurance Risk Classification," *Virginia Law Review* 71 (1985): 403-451. Bryce Christensen, "The Costly Retreat from Marriage," *The Public Interest* No. 91 (1988): 59-66.

2   I.M.A. Joung et al., "Health Behaviors Explain Part of the Differences in Self-Reported Health Associated with Partner/Marital States in the Netherlands," *Journal of Epidemiology and Community Health* 49 (1995): 482-488.

3   Susan Kennedy et al., "Immunological Consequences of Acute and Chronic Stressors: Mediating role of Interpersonal Relationship," *British Journal of Medical Psychology* 61 (1988): 77-85. Myriam Khlat, Catherine Sermet, and Annick Le Pape, "Women's health in relation with their family and work roles: France in the early 1990s," *Social Science & Medicine* 50 (2000): 1807-1825.

4   Ellen Eliason Kisker and Noreen Goldman, "Perils of Single Life and Benefits of Marriage," *Social Biology* 34 (1987): 135-151. Ingrid Waldron, Christopher C. Weiss, and Mary Elizabeth Hughes, "Marital Status Effects on Health: Are There Differences Between Never-Married Women and Divorced and Separated Women?," *Social Science & Medicine* 45 (1997): 1387-1397.

5   Allan Carlson, "Toward a Family-Centered Theory of Taxation," *The Family in America* 12 (January 1998): 1-8. Thomas J. Espenshade and Joseph J. Minarik, "Demographic Implications of the 1986 US Tax Reform," *Population and Development Review* 13 (1987): 115-127. Eugene Steuerle, "The Tax Treatment of

Households of Different Size," in *Taxing the Family*, ed. R.G. Penner (Washington: American Enterprise Institute, 1983), 72-75.

6   Edward J. McCaffery, "The Political Liberal Case Against the Estate Tax," *Philosophy and Public Affairs* 23 (1994): 281-312. Richard A. Musgrave, "Is a Property Tax on Housing Regressive?" *The American Economic Review* 64 (1974): 222-229. United States Senate, 107th Congress, 1st Session, *Easing the Family Tax Burden*, Hearing Before the Committee on Finance, 8 March 2001 (Washington: U.S. Government Office, 2001).

7   Eileen Boris, "Crafts Shop or Sweatshop? The Uses and Abuses of Craftmanship in Twentieth-Century America," *Journal of Design History* 2 (1989): 175-192. Charles Davenport, Michael D. Boehlje, and David B.H. Martin, "Taxes and the Family Farm," *Proceedings of the Academy of Political Science* 34 (1982): 112-121.

8   Bryce Christensen, "For Profit or for Posterity? The Unique Legacy of America's Family Businesses," *The Family in America* 18 (July 2004): 1-8. Robert E. Kraut and Patricia Grambsch, "Home-Based White Collar Employment: Lessons from the 1980 Census," *Social Forces* 66 (1987): 410-426.

9   Richard M. Vogel, "Relocation Subsidies: Regional Growth Policy or Corporate Welfare?" *Review of Radical Political Economics* 32 (2000): 437-457. Robert Weissman, "Corporate Welfare Challenge," *Multinational Monitor* (January/February 2000): 20-26.

10   Robert O. Baldwin, "Femininity-Masculinity of Blacks and Whites Over a Fourteen-Year Period," *Psychological Reports* 60 (1987): 455-458. Allan Carlson, "The Androgyny Hoax," *Family Questions* (New Brunswick: Transaction, 1988): 29-47. Alice H. Eagley, "The Science and Politics of Comparing Men and Women," *American Psychologist* 50 (1995): 145-158. J. Richard Udry, "Biological Limits of Gender Construction," *American Sociological Review* 65 (2000): 443-57.

11   Carol Flake-Hobson, Patsy Skeen, and Bryan E. Robinson, "Review of Theories and Research concerning Sex-Role Development and Androgyny with Suggestions for Teachers," *Family Relations* 29 (1980): 155-162. The National Project of Women in Education, U.S. Department of Health, Education, and Welfare, *Taking Sexism Out of Education* (Washington: U.S. Government Printing Office, 1978). Mary Ellen Verheyden-Hilliard, *Reducing Sex Stereotyping in Career Education: Some Promising Approaches to Persistent Problems* (Washington: U.S. Government Printing Office, 1979).

12   Allan Carlson, "Gender, Children, and Social Labor: Transcending the 'Family Wage' Dilemma," *Journal of Social Issues* 52 (1996): 137-161.

13   Mark Evan Edwards, "Uncertainty and the Rise of the Work-Family Dilemma," *Journal of Marriage and the Family* 61(2001): 183-196. Allan Carlson, *The 'American Way': Familiy and Community in the Shaping of the American Identity* (Wilmington: ISI Books, 2003), 153-160.

14   Carlson, *The 'American Way'*, 153-160.

15   William Lowe Boyd, "Balancing Public and Private Schools: The Australian Experience and American Implications," *Educational Evaluation and Policy Analysis* 9.3 (1987): 183-198. Dick Neal, "How Vouchers Could Change the Market for Education," *The Journal of Economic Perspectives* 16.4 (2002): 25-44. E.G. West, "The Burdens of Monopoly: Classical versus Neoclassical," *Southern Economic Journal* 44 (1978): 829-845.

16   Douglas Besharov, "The Need to Narrow the Grounds for State Intervention," in *Protecting Children from Abuse and Neglect*, ed. Douglas Besharov (Springfield: Charles Thomas, 1988): 62-88. Joseph Goldstein, Anna Freud, and Albert Solnit, *Before the Best Interests of the Child* (New York: Free Press, 1979): 24-25, 136-137.

17   Martin Guggenheim, "Child Protection, Foster Care, and Termination of Parental Rights," *What's Wrong With Children's Rights* (Cambridge: Harvard University Press, 2005): 174-212.

18   Hans Sebald, "Witch Children: The Myth of the Innocent Child," *Issues in Child Abuse Accusation* 8 (1996): 179-186. Frederic N. Silverman, "Child Abuse: The Conflict of Underdetection and Overreporting," *Pediatrics* 80 (1987): 442. San Diego Grand Jury, "Child Sexual Abuse, Assault, And Molest Issues," Report No. 8, 29 June 1992.

19   Jennifer Nerissa Davis and Martin Daly, "Evolutionary Theory and the Human Family," *The Quarterly Review of Biology* 72 (1997): 407-435.

20   David Herlihy, "Biology and History: The Triumph of Monogamy," *Journal of Interdisciplinary History* 25 (1995): 571-583. Umberto Melotti, "Towards a New Theory of the Origin of the Family," *Current Anthropology* 22 (1981): 625-638. Abraham Sagi et al., "'Sleeping Out of Home in a Kibbutz Communal Arrangement: It Makes a Difference for Infant-Mother Attachment," *Child Development* 65 (1994): 992-1004.

21   E. Franklin Frazier, "Urbanization and the Negro Family," in *The Negro and the City*, ed. Richard B. Sherman (Englewood Cliffs: Prentice Hall, 1970): 109-112. Daniel Patrick Moynihan, *The Negro Family: The Case for National Action* [1965] in *The Moynihan Report and the Politics of Controversy*, ed. Lee Rainwater and William L. Yancey (Cambridge: Massachusetts Institute of Technology, 1967), 50-105. Charles Murray, "Does Welfare Bring More Babies?" *Public Interest* No. 115 (1994): 17-30.

22   Allan C. Carlson, *From Cottage to Work Station: The Family's Search for Social Harmony in the Industrial Age* (San Francisco: Ignatius, 1993). Andrew Cherlin, "The Deinstitutionalization of Marriage," *Journal of Marriage and Family* 66 (2004): 848-863. Terry Arendell, "The Social Self as Gendered: A Masculinist Discourse of Divorce," *Symbolic Interaction* 15 (1992): 151-181.

23   Alice H. Eagley, "The Science and Politics of Comparing Men and Women," *American Psychologist* 50 (1995): 145-158. Becky L. Glass and Margaret K. Stolee,

"Family Law in Soviet Russia 1917-1945," *Journal of Marriage and the Family* 49 (1987): 893-901.

24 John L. Esposito, Darrel J. Fasching, and Todd Lewis, *World Religions Today* (New York: Oxford, 2002): 215, 289. Melford E. Spiro, "Religious Symbolism and Social Behavior," *Proceedings of the American Philosophical Society* 113 (1969): 341-349. C.S. Lewis, *The Abolition of Man* (New York: Macmillan and Co., 1974).

25 Nguyen Van Huy, "The Particularity of Popular Beliefs among Ethnic Communities of the Hanhi-Lolo Linguistic Group," *Social Compass* 42 (1995): 301-315. Mei-Lin Lee and T-Hsiung Sun, "The family and demography in contemporary Taiwan," *Journal of Comparative Family Studies* 26 (1995): 101-115.

26 American Academy of Pediatrics Task Force on the Family, "Family Pediatrics," *Pediatrics* 111 Supplement (2003): 1541-1553. Zeng-Yin Chen and Howard B. Kaplan, "Intergenerational Transmission of Constructive Parenting," *Journal of Marriage and the Family* 63 (2001): 17-31. Andrew J. Cherlin, "Going to Extremes: Family Structure, Children's Well-Being, and Social Science," *Demography* 36 (1999): 421-428. Thomas D. Cook et al., "Some Ways in Which Neighborhoods, Nuclear Families, Friendship Groups, and Schools Jointly Affect Changes in Early Adolescent Development," *Child Development* 73 (2002): 1283-1309.

27 Stephen Demuth and Susan L. Brown, "Family Structure, Family Processes, and Adolescent Delinquency: The Significance of Parental Absence Versus Parental Gender," *Journal of Research in Crime and Delinquency* 41 (2004): 58-81. Ross Macmillan and John Hagan, "Violence in the Transition to Adulthood: Adolescent Victimization, Education, and Socioeconomic Attainment in Later Life," *Journal of Research on Adolescence* 14 (2004): 127-158. Jacqueline Scott, "Family, Gender, and Educational Attainment in Britain: A Longitudinal Study," *Journal of Comparative Family Studies* 35 (2004): 565-589.

28 American Academy of Pediatrics Task Force on the Family, "Family Pediatrics," 1541-1553.

29 Nicole J. Cronk et al., "Risk for Separation Anxiety Disorder Among Girls: Paternal Absence, Socioeconomic Disadvantage, and Genetic Vulnerability," *Journal of Abnormal Psychology* 113 (2004): 237-247.

30 David H. Demo and Alan C. Acock, "Family Structure, Family Process, and Adolescent Well-Being," *Journal of Research on Adolescence* 6 (1996): 457-488. Demuth and Brown, "Family Structure, Family Processes, and Adolescent Delinquency," 58-81.

31 Bruce J. Ellis et al., "Quality of Early Family Relationships and Individual Differences in the Timing of Pubertal Maturation in Girls: A Longitudinal Test of an Evolutionary Model," *Journal of Personality and Social Psychology* 77 (1999): 387-401.

32 K.A.S. Wickrama et al., "Linking Early Social Risks to Impaired Physical Health during the Transition to Adulthood," *Journal of Health and Social Behavior* 44 (2003): 61-74.

33   Cynthia C. Harper and Sara S. McLanahan, "Father Absence and Youth In-
     carceration," *Journal of Research on Adolescence* 14 (2004): 369-397.
34   P. Lindsay Chase Lansdale, Andrew J. Cherlin, and Kathleen F. Kiernan, "The
     Long-Term Effects of Parental Divorce on the Mental Health of Young Adults:
     A Developmental Perspective," *Child Development* 66 (1995): 1614-1634.
35   Jeanne M. Hilton and Stephan Desrochers, "Children's Behavior Problems
     in Single-Parent and Married-Parent Families: Development of a Predictive
     Model," *Journal of Divorce & Remarriage* 37 (2003): 13-34. Ellen L. Lipman et al.,
     "Child Well-Being in Single-Mother Families," *Journal of the American Academy
     of Child and Adolescent Psychiatry* 41 (2002): 75-82. Suet-Ling Pong, "Family
     Structure, School Context, and Eighth Grade Math and Reading Achievement,"
     Journal of Marriage and the Family 59 (1997): 734-746.
36   Karen Seccombe, "Families in Poverty in the 1990s: Trends, Causes, Conse-
     quences, and Lessons Learned," *Journal of Marriage and the Family* 62 (2000):
     1094-1113. David Wood, "Effect of Child and Family Poverty on Child Health
     in the United States," *Pediatrics* 112 (2003): 707-212.
37   American Academy of Pediatrics Task Force on the Family, "Family Pediatrics,"
     1541-1553. Bruce J. Ellis and Judy Garber, "Psychosocial Antecedents of Varia-
     tion in Girls' Pubertal Timing: Maternal Depression, Stepfather Presence, and
     Family Stress," *Child Development* 71 (2000): 485-501. John Hagan and Holly
     Foster, "S/He's a Rebel: Toward a Sequential Stress Theory of Delinquency and
     Gendered Pathways to Disadvantage in Emerging Adulthood," *Social Forces* 82
     (2003): 53-86.
38   William Jeynes, "A Longitudinal Analysis of the Effects of Remarriage Follow-
     ing Divorce on the Academic Achievement of Adolescents," *Journal of Divorce
     & Remarriage* 33 (2000): 131-148. Pong, "Family Structure, School Context, and
     Eighth Grade Math and Reading Achievement," *Journal of Marriage and the
     Family* 59 (1997): 734-746.
39   Paul Cameron and Kirk Cameron, "Children of Homosexual Parents Report
     Childhood Difficulties," *Psychological Reports* 90 (2002): 71-82.
40   Lynn D. Wardle, "The Potential Impact of Homosexual Parenting on Children,"
     University of Illinois Law Review (1997): 833-919.
41   Thomas M. Achenbach et al., "National Survey of Problems and Competencies
     Among Four- to Sixteen-Year-Olds: Parents Reports for Normative and Clinical
     Samples," *Monographs for the Society for Research in Child Development, Serial
     No. 225*, 56.3 (1991): 68-93. American Academy of Pediatrics Task Force on the
     Family, *Family Pediatrics*: 1541-1553.
42   Susan L. Brown, "Family Structure and Child Well-Being: The Significance
     of Parental Cohabitation," Journal of Marriage and Family 66 (2004): 351-367.
     Thomas DeLeire and Ariel Kalil, "How Do Cohabiting Couples With Children
     Spend Their Money?" *Journal of Marriage and Family* 67 (2005): 286-295.

43 Ora Aviezer, Sagi Abraham, and Marinus va Ijzendoom, "Balancing the Family and the Collective in Raising Children: Why Communal Sleeping in Kibbutzim Was Predestined to End," *Family Process* 41 (2002): 435-454.

44 Abraham Sagi et al., ""Sleeping Out of Home in a Kibbutz Communal Arrangement: It Makes a Difference for Infant-Mother Attachment," *Child Development* 65 (1994): 992-1004. Miri Scharf, "A 'Natural Experiment' in Childrearing: Ecologies and Adolescents' Attachment and Separation Representations," *Child Development* 72 (2001): 236-251.

6 *Gifts of the Natural Family*

1 American Academy of Pediatrics Task Force on the Family, "Family Pediatrics," *Pediatrics* 111 Supplement (2003): 1541-1553. John G. Guidubaldi and Helen Cleminshaw, "Divorce, Family Health, and Child Adjustment," *Family Relations* 34 (1985): 35-41. James L. Lynch, *The Broken Heart: The Medical Consequences of Loneliness* (New York: Basic, 1977), 78-80. David Wood, "Effect of Child and Family Poverty on Child Health in the United States," *Pediatrics* 112 (2003): 207-212. Gwendolyn E.P. Zahner and Constantine Daskalakis, "Factors Associated with Mental Health, General Health, and School-Based Service Use for Child Psychopathology," *American Journal of Public Health* 87 (1997): 1440-1448.

2 Cheryl Buehler and Kay Pasley, "Family Boundary Ambiguity, Marital Status, and Child Adjustment," *Journal of Early Adolescence* 20 (2000): 281-308. Vincent J. Roscigno, "Family/ School Inequality and African-American/Hispanic Achievement," *Social Problems* 47 (2000): 266-290. Jacqueline Scott, "Family, Gender, and Educational Attainment in Britain: A Longitudinal Study," *Journal of Comparative Family Studies* 35 (2004): 565-589.

3 Thomas D. Cook et al., "Some Ways in Which Neighborhoods, Nuclear Families, Friendship Groups, and Schools Jointly Affect Changes in Early Adolescent Development," *Child Development* 73 (2002): 1283-1309. Ross Macmillan and John Hagan, "Violence in the Transition to Adulthood: Adolescent Victimization, Education, and Socioeconomic Attainment in Later Life," *Journal of Research on Adolescence* 14 (2004): 127-158. Mary Ann Powell and Toby L. Parcel, "Effects of Family Structure on the Earnings Attainment Process: Differences by Gender," *Journal of Marriage and the Family* 59 (1997): 419-433.

4 Yuaureng Hu and Noreen Goldman, "Mortality Differentials by Marital Status: An International Comparison," *Demography* 27 (1990): 233-250. Myriam Khlat, Catherine Sermet, and Annick Le Pape, "Women's health in relation with their family and work roles: France in the early 1990s," *Social Science & Medicine* 50 (2000): 1807-1825. Ellen Eliason Kisker and Noreen Goldman, "Perils of Single Life and Benefits of Marriage," *Social Biology* 34 (1987): 135-151. Thomas Rutledge et al., "Social Networks and Marital Status Predict Mortality in Older Women:

Prospective Evidence from the Study of Osteoporotic Fractures," *Psychosomatic Medicine* 65 (2003): 688-694. Paul D. Sortie, Eric Backlund, and Jacob B. Keller, "U. S. Mortality by Economic, Demographic, and Social Characteristics: The National Longitudinal Mortality Study," *American Journal of Public Health* 85 (1995): 949-956. Leslie R. Martin, et al. "Longevity Following the Experience of Parental Divorce," *Social Science Journal* 61 (2005): 2177-2189.

5   Thomas A. Hirschl, Joyce Altobelli, and Mark R. Rank, "Does Marriage Increase the Odds of Affluence? Exploring the Life Course Probabilities," *Journal of Marriage and Family* 65 (2003): 927-938. Janet Wilmoth and Gregor Koso, "Does Marital History Matter? Marital Status and Wealth Outcomes Among Preretirement Adults," *Journal of Marriage and Family* 64 (2002): 254-268.

6   Daniel T. Lichter, Deborah Roempke Graefe, and J. Brian Brown, "Is Marriage a Panacea? Union Formation Among Economically Disadvantaged Unwed Mothers," *Social Problems* 50(2003): 60-86. United States Commission on Civil Rights, *The Economic Status of Black Women: An Exploratory Investigation*, Staff Report, Oct. 1990: 96-116.

7   Corey L. M. Keyes, "The Mental Health Continuum: From Languishing to Flourishing in Life," *Journal of Health and Social Behavior* 43 (2002): 207-222.

8   Harsha N. Mookherjee, "Marital Status, Gender and Perception of 'Well-Being,'" *The Journal of Social Psychology* 137 (1997): 95-105. Steven Stack and J. Ross Eshleman, "Marital Status and Happiness: a 17-Nation Study," *Journal of Marriage and the Family* 60 (1998): 527-536.

9   John G. Guidubaldi and Helen Cleminshaw, "Divorce, Family Health, and Child Adjustment," *Family Relations* 34 (1985): 35-41. Margaret Whitehead, Bo Burstrom, and Finn Diderichsen, "Social policies and the pathways to inequalities in health: a comparative analysis of lone mothers in Britain and Sweden," *Social Science and Medicine* 50 (2000): 255-270.

10   Lorraine Davies, "Significant Life Experiences and Depression Among Single and Married Mothers," *Journal of Marriage and the Family* 59 (1997): 294-309. Hilde Mausner-Dorsch and William W. Eaton, "Psychosocial Work Environment and Depression: Epidemiologic Assessment of the Demand Control Model," *American Journal of Public Health* 90 (2000) : 1765-1770. Peggy A. Thoits, "Gender and Marital Status Differences in Control and Distress: Common Stress versus Unique Stress Explanations," *Journal of Health and Social Behavior* 28 (1987): 7-22. Allan V. Horwitz, Helene Raskin White, and Sandra Howell-White, "Becoming Married and Mental Health: A Longitudinal Study of a Cohort of Young Adults," *Journal of Marriage and the Family* 58 (1997): 895-907.

11   John E. Murray, "Marital Protection and Marital Selection: Evidence from a Historical-Prospective Sample of American Men," *Demography* 37 (2000): 511-521. Paul D. Sorlie, Eric Backlund, and Jacob B. Keller, "U. S. Mortality by

Economic, Demographic, and Social Characteristics: The National Longitudinal Mortality Study," *American Journal of Public Health* 85 (1995): 949-956.

12   Donald G. Dutton, "Patriarchy and Wife Assault: The Ecological Fallacy," *Violence and Victims* 9 (1994): 167-182. Lisa K. Walder-Haugrud, Linda Vaden Gratch, and Brian Magruder, "Victimization and Perpetration Rates of Violence in Gay and Lesbian Relationships: Gender Issues Explored," *Violence and Victims* 12 (1997): 173-184. Terry Huffman et al., "Gender Differences and Factors Related to the Disposition Toward Cohabitation," *Family Therapy* 21 (1994): 171-184. Jan E. Stets, "Cohabiting and Marital Aggression: The Role of Social Isolation," *Journal of Marriage and the Family* 53 (1991): 669-680. Kersti Yllo and Murray Straus, "Interpersonal Violence Among Married and Cohabiting Couples," *Family Relations* 30 (1981): 339-347.

13   Jan E. Stets and Murray A. Straus, "The Marriage License as a Hitting License: A Comparison of Assaults in Dating, Cohabiting, and Married Couples," Paper presented at the 1988 Meeting of the American Sociological Association, VB20F. PSS, VB119, 8 July 1988. Maria Testa, Jennifer A. Livingston, and Kenneth E. Leonard, "Women's substance abuse and experiences of intimate partner violence: A longitudinal investigation among a community sample," *Addictive Behaviors* 28 (2003): 1649-1664.

14   Martin Daly and Margo Wilson, "Child Abuse and Other Risks of Not Living With Both Parents," *Ethology and Sociobiology* 6 (1985): 197-209. Joy L. Lightcap, Jeffrey A. Kurland, and Robert L Burgess, "Child Abuse: A Test of Some Predictions From Evolutionary Theory," *Ethology and Sociobiology* 3 (1982): 63-68. Richard J. Gelles, "Child Abuse and Violence in Single-Parent Families: Parent Absence and Economic Deprivation," *American Journal of Orthopsychiatry* 59 (1989): 492-501.

15   David Finkelhor et al., "Sexually Abused Children in a National Survey of Parents: Methodological Issues," *Child Abuse and Neglect* 21 (1997): 1-9.

16   David Finkelhor et al., "Sexual Abuse in a National Survey of Adult Men and Women: Prevalence, Characteristics, and Risk Factors," *Child Abuse and Neglect* 14 (1990): 19-28.

17   Ross Macmillan and John Hagan, "Violence in the Transition to Adulthood: Adolescent Victimization, Education, and Socioeconomic Attainment in Later Life," *Journal of Research on Adolescence* 14 (2004): 127-158.

18   Bryce Christensen, "For Profit or for Posterity? The Unique Legacy of America's Family Businesses," *The Family in America* 18 (July 2004): 1-8. Ronald Dore, "Goodwill and the Spirit of Market Capitalism," *British Journal of Market Capitalism* 34 (1983): 462-480. Charles Delheim, "The Creation of a Company Culture: Cadburys, 1861-1931," *American Historical Review* 92 (1987): 14-43. Terry A. Beehr, John A. Drexler, Jr., and Sonja Faulkner, "Working in Small Family Businesses: Empirical Comparisons to Non-Family Businesses," *Journal of Organizational Behavior* 18 (1997): 297-310.

19 Michael L. Blim, "Introduction: The Emerging Global Factory and Anthro-
    pology," and Frances Abrahamer Rothstein, "Conclusion: New Waves and
    Old-Industrialization Labor, and the Struggle for the New World Order," in
    Anthropology of the Global Factory, ed. by Frances Abrahamer Rothstein and
    Michael L. Blim (New York: Bergin & Garvey, 1992): 1-30, 238-246. Stuart
    Ewen, *Captains of Consciousness: Advertising and the Social Roots of the Consumer
    Culture* (New York: McGraw Hill, 1976): 161-164. Andrew Kakabadse and Nada
    Kakabadse, *The Geopolitics of Governance: The Impact of Contrasting Philosophies*
    (New York: Palgrave, 2001). Sharon M. Keigher and Christine T. Lowery, "The
    Sickening Implications of Globalization," *Health and Social Work* 23 (1998):
    153-158. David C. Korten, *When Corporations Rule the World* (West Hartford:
    Kumarian/Berrett-Koehler, 1995): 1-23, 215-220.

20 Wendy A. Goldberg, Ellen Greenberger, and Stacy K. Nagel, "Employment and
    Achievement: Mothers' Work Involvement in Relation to Children's Achieve-
    ment Behaviors and Mothers' Parenting Behaviors," *Child Development* 67 (1996):
    1512-1527. Matthijs Kalmijn, "Mother's Occupational Status and Children's
    Schooling," *American Sociological Review* 59 (1994): 257-275.

21 Chandra Muller, "Maternal Employment, Parent Involvement, and Mathematics
    Achievement Among Adolescents," *Journal of Marriage and the Family* 57 (1995):
    85-100. Frank P. Stafford, "Women's Work, Sibling Competition, and Children's
    School Performance," *The American Economic Review* 77 (1987): 972-980.

22 Valerie Kincade Oppenheimer, "Women's Rising Employment and the Future
    of the Family in Industrial Societies," *Population and Development Review* 20
    (1994): 293-336. Jennifer Roeback Morse, *Love & Economics: Why the Laissez-
    Faire Family Doesn't Work* (Dallas: Spence, 2001): 3-22.

23 Samantha K. Ammons and William T. Markham, "Working at Home: Experi-
    ences of Skilled White-Collar Workers," *Sociological Spectrum* 24 (2004): 191-239.
    Linda Duxbury, Christopher Higgins, and Derrick Neufeld, "Telework and the
    Balance between Work and Family: Is Telework Part of the Problem or Part of
    the Solution?" in *The Virtual Workplace*, ed. M. Igbaria and M. Tan (Hershey:
    Idea Group Publishing, 1998): 218-255. Jeffrey E. Hill, Alan J. Hawkins, and
    Brent C. Miller, "Work and Family in the Virtual Office," *Family Relations* 45
    (1996): 293-301.

24 Helen Rose Ebaugh, "Presidential Address 2001: Return of the Sacred: Re-
    integrating Religion in the Social Sciences," *Journal for the Scientific Study of
    Religion* 41 (2002): 385-395. Darwin L. Thomas and Marie Cornwall, "Religion
    and Family in the 1980s: Discovery and Development," *Journal of Marriage and
    the Family* 52 (1990): 983-992. Edward O. Wilson, *Sociobiology: The New Synthesis*
    (Cambridge: Harvard University Press, 1975): 167-168, 561-562.

25 Daniel N. Spicer, "World View and Abortion Beliefs: A Replication of Luker's
    Implicit Hypothesis," *Sociological Inquiry* 64 (1994): 114-126. Steven Stack, Ira

Wasserman, Augustine Kposowa, "The Effects of Religion and Feminism on Suicide Ideology: An Analysis of National Survey Data," *Journal for the Scientific Study of Religion* 33 (1994): 110-121.

26 Sanjiv Gupta, Pamela J. Smock, and Wendy D. Manning, "Moving Out: Transition to Nonresidence Among Resident Fathers in the United States, 1968-1997," *Journal of Marriage and Family* 66 (2004): 627-638. U.S. Census Bureau, "Living Arrangements of Children Under 18 Years Old: 1960 to Present," Table CH-1, 15 Sept. 2004, *Families and Living Arrangements*, at <http://www.census.gov/population/www/socdemo/hh-fam.html> (10 June 2005).

27 American Academy of Pediatrics Task Force on the Family, "Family Pediatrics," 1541-1553. Claudia J. Coulton and Shanta Pandey, "Geographic Concentration of Poverty and Risk to Children in Urban Neighborhoods," *American Behavioral Scientist* 35 (1992): 238-257. David Courtwright, *Violent Land: Single Men and Social Disorder from the Frontier to the Inner City* (Cambridge: Harvard University Press, 1996): 240-280.

28 David T. Ellwood, "Anti-Poverty Policy for Families in the Next Century: From Welfare to Work—and Worries," *Journal of Economic Perspectives* 14 (2000): 187-198.

29 Cynthia C. Harper and Sara S. McLanahan, "Father Absence and Youth Incarceration," *Journal of Research on Adolescence* 14 (2004): 369-397. Kathleen Mullan Harris, Greg J. Duncan, and Johanne Boisjoly, "Evaluating the Role of 'Nothing to Lose' Attitudes on Risky Behavior in Adolescence," *Social Forces* 80 (2002): 1005-1039.

30 Margaret McHugh, "Child Abuse in a Sea of Neglect: The Inner-City Child," *Pediatric Annals* 21 (1992): 504-507. Robert D. Plotnick et al., "Inequality and poverty in the United States: The twentieth-century record," *Focus* 19.3 (1998): 7-14.

31 Howard M. Bahr and Kathleen S. Bahr, "Families and Self-Sacrifice: Alternative Models and Meanings for Family Theory," *Social Forces* 79 (2001): 1231-1258. John C. Caldwell and Thomas Schindlmayr, "Explanations of the fertility crisis in modern societies: A search for commonalities," *Population Studies* 57 (2003): 241-263. Michele Hoffnung, "Wanting It All: Career, Marriage, and Motherhood During College-Educated Women's 20s," *Sex Roles* 50 (2004): 711-723.

7 Introspection and Confession

1 Barbara Dafoe Whitehead, "What Families Must do for Children," *The Chicago Tribune* (October 1, 1991).

2 See: Chapter 5, "In Defense of the Natural Family," in: Doris Buss and Didi Herman, *Globalizing Family Values: The Christian Right in International Politics* (Minneapolis: University of Minnesota Press, 2003).

8   *A Natural Family Policy*

1   Louis de Bonald, *On Divorce*, trans. and ed. By Nicholas Davidson (New Brunswick, NJ: Transaction, 1992 [1801]): 36-37.

2   Edmund Burke, *Reflections on the French Revolution* (London: J.M. Dent & Sons, 1955 [1790]): 44.

3   Abraham Kuyper, "Maranatha" [Speech to the 1891 convention of the Anti-Revolutionary Party held in Utrecht], in James D. Bratt, ed., *Abraham Kuyper: A Centennial Reader* (Grand Rapids, MI: William B. Eerdmans, 1998): 212.

4   Abraham Kuyper, "Uniformity: The Curse of Modern Life, [22 April 1869]," in Bratt, *Abraham Kuyper: A Centennial Reader*, p. 32.

5   Kuyper, "Maranatha," 225-26.

6   A role described and praised by sociologist Talcott Parsons in "An Analytical Approach to the Theory of Social Stratification," *Essays in Sociological Theory* (Glencoe, IL: The Free Press, 1949): 174.

7   The full text of this report can be found in: Lee Rainwater and William L. Yancy, eds., *The Moynihan Report and the Politics of Controversy* (Cambridge, MA: MIT Press, 1967).

8   Lawrence M. Rudner, "Scholastic Achievement and Demographic Characteristics of Home School Students in 1998," *Education Policy Analysis Archives* 7 (23 March 1999): 7-8, 12.

9   Leslie Whittington, "Taxes and the Family: The Impact of the Tax Exemption for Dependents on Marital Fertility," *Demography* 29 (May 1992): 220-21; and L.A. Whittington, J. Alan, and H.E. Peters, "Fertility and the Personal Exemption: Implicit Pronatalist Policy in the United States," *The American Economic Review* 80 (June 1990): 545-56.

10   Allan Carlson, "Separation and Cooperation: Perspectives from the USA and Europe." Paper for The Cooperation of Church and State Conference, The Centre for Cultural Renewal, Calgary, Alberta, June 8-9, 2006.

11   See: F. Althous, "Differences in Fertility of Catholics and Protestants Are Related to Timing and Prevalence of Marriage," *Family Planning Perspectives* 24 (Sept/Oct. 1992).

12   Steven E. Rhoads, *Taking Sex Differences Seriously* (San Francisco: Encounter Books, 2004).

13   Jane Lawler Dye, "Fertility of American Women: June 2004," *Current Population Reports*, p20-555, U.S. Census Bureau, December 2005.

14   Phillip Longman, "The Return of Patriarchy," *Foreign Policy* (March/April 2006).

15   For a more detailed list of policy prescriptions and their specific justifications, see: Allan Carlson, *Fractured Generations: Crafting a Family Policy for Twenty-First Century America* (New Brunswick, NJ: Transaction, 2006): 135-40.

16 See: "The Child-Care 'Crisis' and Its Remedies," *Family Policy Review* 1 (Fall 2003): 1-159.
17 See: Charles F. Hohm, et al, "A Reappraisal of the Social Security-Fertility Hypothesis: A Bidirectional Approach," *The Social Science Journal* 23 (1986): 163; Isaac Ehrlich and Francis T. Lui, "Social Security, the Family, and Economic Growth," *Economic Inquiry* 36 (July 1998): 404; and Allan Carlson, "Making Social Security Reform Family Friendly," a Family Policy Lecture for the Family Research Council, February 23, 2005.

Index